VISUAL TIMELINES LIFE ON EARTH

FROM THE FIRST CELLS TO THE MODERN WORLD

ANNE ROONEY

ILLUSTRATED BY
VIOLET TOBACCO

ARCTURUS

WHO'S ON THE COVER?

These are the animals on the cover, and a list of pages where you can find more information about them.

1 *Dimetrodon*, page 51
2 *Morganucodon*, page 63
3 *Smilodon*, page 113
4 Dinosaurs, pages 66–87
5 Human, pages 112, 114–115, 117, and 122
6 *Cloudina*, page 20
7 Bacteria, pages 13 and 14
8 Woolly mammoth, page 121
9 Fishapod, page 38

ARCTURUS

This edition published in 2023 by Arcturus Publishing Limited
26/27 Bickels Yard, 151–153 Bermondsey Street,
London SE1 3HA

Author: Anne Rooney
Illustrator: Violet Tobacco
Designer: Trudi Webb
Editors: Felicity Forster and Becca Clunes
Managing Designer: Jessica Holliland
Managing Editor: Joe Harris

ISBN: 978-1-3988-2069-2
CH010049US
Supplier 29, Date 0123, PI 00001969

Printed in China

CONTENTS

4 INTRODUCTION

8 **CHAPTER 1: COMING TO LIFE**
10 4.6–4.4 BILLION YEARS AGO
12 LIFE STARTS
14 4.4–2.1 BILLION YEARS AGO
16 2.1 BILLION–720 MILLION YEARS AGO
18 719–556 MILLION YEARS AGO
20 555–535 MILLION YEARS AGO
22 534–501 MILLION YEARS AGO
24 ANIMALS FOR THE FUTURE

26 **CHAPTER 2: THE MOVE TO LAND**
28 500–445 MILLION YEARS AGO
30 CATASTROPHE!
32 444–420 MILLION YEARS AGO
34 419–390 MILLION YEARS AGO
36 FROM ROCK TO FOREST
38 389–360 MILLION YEARS AGO
40 359–315 MILLION YEARS AGO
42 FROM TREES TO COAL
44 314–300 MILLION YEARS AGO

46 **CHAPTER 3: THE RISE OF REPTILES**
48 A GOOD EGG
50 299–276 MILLION YEARS AGO
52 275–252 MILLION YEARS AGO
54 GOODBYE TO ALL THESE
56 251–245 MILLION YEARS AGO
58 BACK TO THE WATER
60 244–220 MILLION YEARS AGO
62 219–201 MILLION YEARS AGO
64 THE RISE OF DINOSAURS

66 **CHAPTER 4: AGE OF DINOSAURS**
68 201–170 MILLION YEARS AGO
70 TAKE TO THE SKIES
72 169–156 MILLION YEARS AGO
74 155–145 MILLION YEARS AGO
76 GROWING ALIKE, GROWING APART
78 144–116 MILLION YEARS AGO
80 FLYING WITH FEATHERS
82 115–81 MILLION YEARS AGO
84 80–65.5 MILLION YEARS AGO
86 A SUDDEN END

88 **CHAPTER 5: MAMMALS TAKE OVER**
90 65.5–56 MILLION YEARS AGO
92 MAMMALS CREEP FROM THE SHADOWS
94 55–45 MILLION YEARS AGO
96 44–35 MILLION YEARS AGO
98 34–24 MILLION YEARS AGO
100 GRASSLANDS AND GRAZERS
102 23–11 MILLION YEARS AGO
104 10–3 MILLION YEARS AGO
106 OUT OF THE TREES

108 **CHAPTER 6: A WORLD OF CHANGE**
110 ON THE MOVE
112 3–1 MILLION YEARS AGO
114 OUT OF AFRICA
116 1 MILLION–300,000 YEARS AGO
118 300,000–80,000 YEARS AGO
120 A WORLD SHAPED BY ICE
122 80,000–12,000 YEARS AGO
124 10,000 BCE–NOW
126 ON THE BRINK

128 **INDEX**

INTRODUCTION

Our planet is teeming with life, from deep oceans to forests, deserts, and mountains, and from the air above us to the rocks beneath us. Organisms (living things) have found ways to survive in every corner of Earth. There is a huge variety of living things, ranging from those too small to see without a microscope to fungi that cover several square kilometers.

Earth's largest living structure, the Great Barrier Reef

Williamsonia, a Jurassic seed plant

A long prehistory

All life on Earth today has evolved from earlier life forms, beginning around four billion (4,000,000,000) years ago. Evolution involves changing over time. Organisms evolve to become or remain well suited to the conditions they live in. They evolve in response to pressures and challenges, like a change in climate or the arrival of a new predator that wants to eat them. The individuals best suited to their living conditions survive and breed, passing on their successful characteristics to the next generation. Individuals less well suited might die or fail to reproduce, so their characteristics are not passed on. This process is called natural selection. Over a long period of time, organisms change and diversify (grow different) until there are many different types, all suited to living in different places and conditions.

Tiktaalik, a fishapod

Euporosteus, an early fish

Ophiacodon, an early reptile

Four-legged land animals have evolved from lobe-finned fish, going through a phase when "fishapods" used their fins to haul themselves up banks onto land and developed the ability to breathe air.

Rocky remains

Much of what we know about organisms that lived in the distant past comes from fossils. These are records left in rock by things long dead. Fossils can be body parts, such as bones, teeth, and claws, that have mineralized over millions of years. Or they can be impressions left where a body has pressed against clay, mud, or sand that has hardened. These impressions can tell us about the soft parts of organisms, such as skin, hair, leaves, and roots—parts that don't generally fossilize. Or fossils can be traces such as burrows or footprints, their shape preserved in the rock.

Meganeura,
an arthropod

Sponge

The hard parts of arthropods fossilize more readily than the soft parts of sponges. There are few fossils more than 550 million years old, since earlier organisms all had soft bodies.

Dying without decaying

Usually, when a plant or animal dies, its body is destroyed. It might be eaten, or broken up by weather and water, or decay. Occasionally, though, it can be fossilized if conditions are just right. If a body falls into water before it is broken up or decays, sediment (sand and soil) can fall over it. As more sediment piles up, heat and pressure slowly turn the sediment to rock. Chemicals in the water change the trapped body, making it hard. It becomes part of the rock but keeps its original shape. If the rock is later revealed, people might find and dig out the fossil.

Rock is laid down in layers, with the oldest the lowest (deepest). The layers can be disrupted by movement of the land, earthquakes, and mountain-building.

How old?

Fossils don't come labeled with their names and dates. People who study fossils, called paleontologists, work to find out what the organisms were like, and when and how they lived. Rock is laid down in layers from the top, so the older rocks are farther down. Where fossils are found tells scientists which organisms are older than others.

Some chemicals gradually change to others as their atoms alter through a process called radioactive decay. This gives scientists a way of measuring the age of rocks that carry fossils. Radiometric dating measures the radioactive decay of atoms in rocks that has taken place over millions of years to give a date.

Rock of ages

Scientists have divided Earth's long history into different named geological ages. The division between ages is often marked by a major event, such as a mass extinction—a time when many types of organisms die out over a relatively short period.

You will see these geological periods referred to in the book. You can check back to this page to see the dates they relate to if you need to.

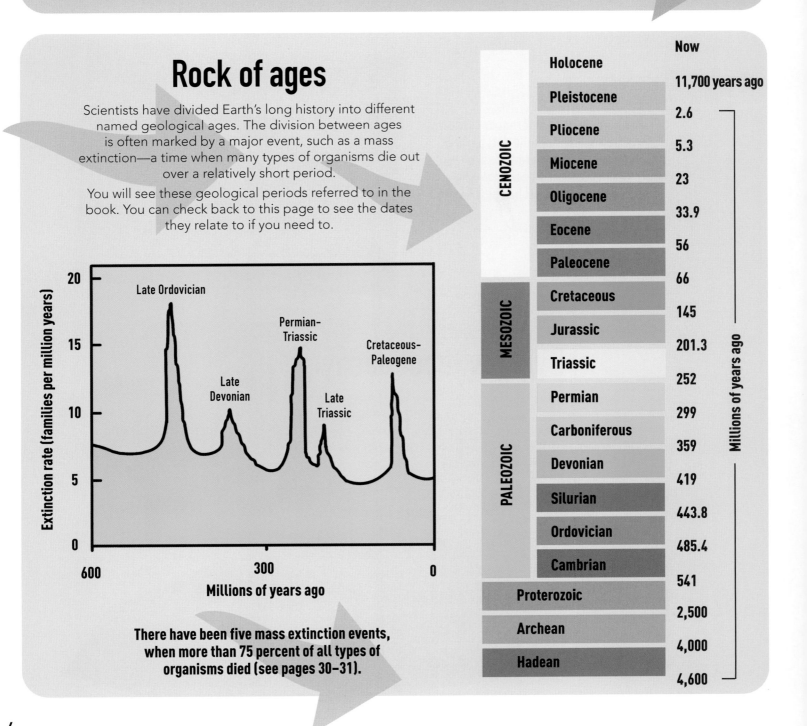

There have been five mass extinction events, when more than 75 percent of all types of organisms died (see pages 30–31).

		Now
CENOZOIC	Holocene	
	Pleistocene	11,700 years ago
	Pliocene	2.6
	Miocene	5.3
	Oligocene	23
	Eocene	33.9
	Paleocene	56
		66
MESOZOIC	Cretaceous	
	Jurassic	145
	Triassic	201.3
		252
PALEOZOIC	Permian	
	Carboniferous	299
	Devonian	359
	Silurian	419
	Ordovician	443.8
	Cambrian	485.4
		541
	Proterozoic	2,500
	Archean	4,000
	Hadean	4,600

Millions of years ago

Extinction rate (families per million years)

Late Ordovician
Permian-Triassic
Late Devonian
Late Triassic
Cretaceous-Paleogene

Millions of years ago

Rare finds

Very few of the organisms that have ever lived have been fossilized. For some types of organism, we have only one or two fossils, and these are often incomplete, with bits missing or broken. If we have a fossil from rock 100 million years ago, we can say the organism lived 100 million years ago—but not when it first appeared or finally died out. It might have existed for just a short time or for 10 or 20 million years.

Fossils of the dinosaur *Parasaurolophus* date from between 77 and 73.5 million years ago. This dinosaur might have appeared earlier or survived later, but it left no other fossils.

Where on Earth?

The landmasses that make up the current continents have moved around Earth over billions of years. The sea level has also gone up and down, so that some of today's seabed was once dry land. Land that is now in Europe has been both under the sea and near the South Pole at some point in Earth's history. At some times the land has been clumped together in a supercontinent, and at others—like now—it is separated by oceans. This affects how animals can move around and how they have evolved.

The world looked very different even just 65 million years ago.

Pretty as a picture

You will find pictures of many organisms in this book, but there is much we don't know about what they actually looked like. When only bones and teeth have survived, we can't tell what kind of skin an animal had, whether it was fat or thin, what color it was, or whether it had fur, feathers, scales, or some other covering. The farther back in time we go, the less certain we can be about how organisms looked, since there are fewer clues from living descendants.

Tupandactylus had a large headcrest that was very possibly brightly patterned, but we can't be sure.

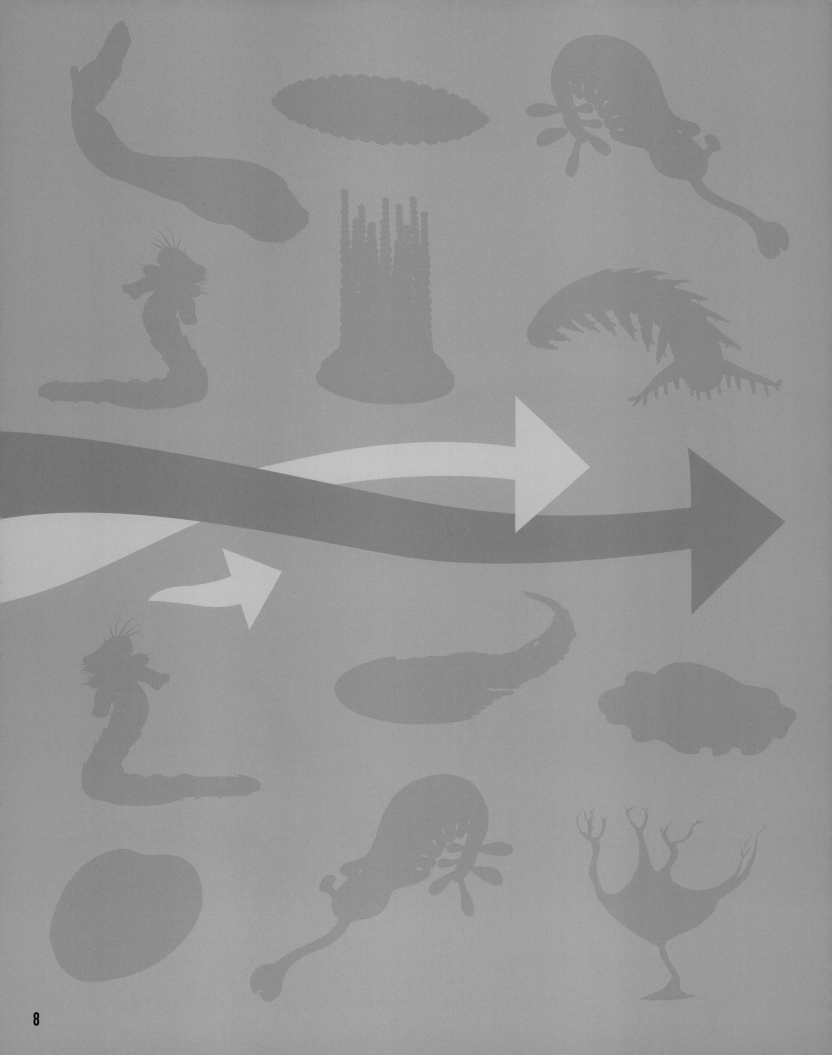

CHAPTER 1

COMING TO LIFE

Earth is the only place that we know to be a home to living things. If we ever find aliens on another planet or moon in our solar system, they are likely to be simple microbes—single-celled organisms that can only be seen with a microscope. Earth's story starts with microbes, too, but a lucky combination of circumstances produced the right conditions for life to flourish, multiply, and grow. The huge diversity of living things on our planet has come from these first tiny beings. Life has changed as our planet has changed, but life has also altered the planet. In a delicate balance of influence, the stuff our planet is made of and its living inhabitants have grown up together. Even the earliest microbes began to change the oceans, rocks, and air around them.

4.6—4.4 BILLION YEARS AGO

Living things need a home, and our home is Earth. Before life could start, Earth needed to form and settle into a fairly stable state. The story began billions of years ago in a vast cloud of dust and gas twisting through space, carrying all the matter that would become the solar system.

4.57 BILLION YEARS AGO

The cloud began to collapse into itself, most of the matter being pulled by gravity to the middle. There, it was squashed together so forcibly that **nuclear fusion** began, starting the glowing Sun.

4.55 BILLION YEARS AGO

The remains of the cloud flattened into a **disk swirling around the new Sun**. As the cloud cooled, tiny bits of rock and ice crashing into each other began to stick together.

The planets formed from the matter swirling around the Sun.

4.6 BILLION YEARS AGO

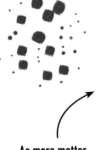

As more matter clumped together, gravity pulled the growing planet into a sphere.

4.54 BILLION YEARS AGO

Earth and the other rocky planets grew by **accretion**—as chunks became larger, their increased gravity attracted even more matter. Earth went around the Sun, also turning on its axis. Gravity, pulling inward on all parts of the surface, made the planet round.

In the growing Earth, gravity squeezed matter together, generating heat that melted the new planet. Molten metal trickled toward the middle between grains of rock, and Earth separated into a thick coat of semi-molten rock around a core of metal. For millions of years, Earth was mostly molten, slowly cooling on the outside, which was exposed to cold space, but scalding within.

4.53 BILLION YEARS AGO

Another growing planet, named **Theia**, smashed into Earth. Theia and a large part of Earth were vaporized (heated until they turned to gas) and thrown out into space. As the vaporized rock cooled, some fell back to Earth, and some became chunks in orbit around Earth. The chunks collected into a great ball of semi-molten rock that became the **Moon**.

The impact of Theia crashing into Earth produced so much heat that rock turned instantly to gas.

4.53–4.52 BILLION YEARS AGO

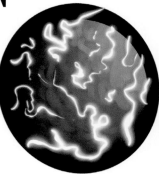

As Earth cooled, the molten rock of the surface hardened. Light material rose from within, and gases, including water vapor, escaped from inside the planet, forming an **atmosphere** (layer of gas).

4.4 BILLION YEARS AGO

Scientists can't be sure whether Earth was hot or cold in the period from 4.4 to 4 billion years ago. The surface would have first been hot, broken up repeatedly by molten rock coming up from within, from 4.6 to 4.4 billion years ago. But it might then have cooled to be something like it is now, with liquid water, some ice, and cool rocks at the surface—or perhaps it remained hot. We don't know.

4.4 BILLION YEARS AGO

Water vapor made clouds that fell as rain. Over millions of years, the rain created **oceans**, which covered most of the surface.

LIFE STARTS

No one knows exactly how, when, or where life first started on Earth. It might have been deep in the sea or perhaps in shallow coastal waters or pools. It could have been any time between 4.5 billion years ago, when the surface hardened, and 3.7 billion years ago, the date of the oldest fossils.

LIFE IN THE WATER

As Earth's surface cooled, liquid water collected in low-lying areas, forming **pools and oceans**. Earth was warmed by the Sun from above and by radioactivity deep within the planet.

In the ocean, **deep-sea vents** are like chimneys that pour scalding hot water out into the surrounding sea. This water, rich in minerals, might have fed microbes that used heat as a source of energy.

Deep-sea vents pouring out mineral-rich hot water are now home to many organisms.

Water that left volcanoes as gas fell as rain, making pools and eventually oceans.

Although living conditions were harsh for the earliest life forms, there are still many organisms that live in extreme environments. Called **"extremophiles,"** they survive in places that are very hot or cold, in acidic liquids, inside rock, and in conditions that contain chemicals poisonous to most other organisms. They range from bacteria far underground to strange, tube-living worms near the vents of underwater volcanoes.

LIFE FROM NOWHERE

In 1952, two American chemists, Harold Urey and Stanley Miller, performed an **experiment to see if living things could emerge in the conditions of early Earth**. They made a "soup" of the chemicals that would have been available in Earth's early oceans and pools, and an atmosphere they thought matched Earth's early atmosphere. Then they used an electric spark as fake lightning to strike their "ocean." They found that chemicals essential to life appeared in the water.

GETTING GOING

Living things need a way to **reproduce** (make copies of themselves). They need to be separated from their environment, and they need a source of energy that they can use. Some chemicals can **copy themselves** if the right ingredients are available, and some other types of chemicals can arrange themselves into tiny hollow pockets that can trap water inside. If self-copying chemicals became trapped inside hollow pockets, that could have been the **starting point that led to the first living things** reproducing and staying separate from their environment. It's one possibility—we can't be sure if it's what actually happened.

Microscopic packages of self-copying chemicals might be how life started.

Modern archaea and bacteria give us a clue as to what the first life might have been like.

FIRST THINGS FIRST

Whichever way the first life appeared, we know that by 3.7 billion years ago there were **microbes**—tiny organisms with single cells. These have been preserved in fossils called stromatolites (see page 15), found in Greenland and Australia.

There are still many single-celled organisms in the world. The first microbes might have been like some of the **archaea** and **bacteria** found today. Now, they come in many different shapes and have different ways of living, but all take chemicals and energy from their environment to fuel their bodies and to reproduce.

WEAVING AN AIRY BLANKET

Earth's early atmosphere was made mostly of carbon dioxide and water vapor. Carbon dioxide is a greenhouse gas—it traps heat near Earth's surface. An atmosphere rich in carbon dioxide would have helped to keep Earth warm at a time when the young Sun gave out much less energy than it does now. It's likely that early microbes helped, too. At least by 3.5 billion years ago, and probably earlier, microbes were making the gas methane from carbon and hydrogen. This is much more powerful than carbon dioxide as a greenhouse gas, and it would have worked even better to trap heat, keeping Earth warm enough for life to thrive.

Earth's atmosphere helped trap the heat of weaker sunlight.

4.4–2.1 BILLION YEARS AGO

Life first emerged somewhere between 4.4 and 3.7 billion years ago. At first, all that lived on Earth were simple, single-celled microbes of a type called "prokaryotes." There are still many prokaryotes in the world today; they are all simple microbes, bacteria, and archaea. One type of early bacteria, cyanobacteria, changed the course of life on Earth forever, making all current life possible.

4.4–3.7 BILLION YEARS AGO

The first simple organisms emerged, the **first life on Earth**.

4.28 BILLION YEARS AGO

The oldest things that might be fossils are **tiny stone tubes** similar to those found on hydrothermal (deep-sea) vents now. They were found in rock in Canada. It's not clear yet whether they are actually fossils.

Tiny tubes of iron-rich mineral found in rock might be evidence of the earliest life on Earth.

4.4 BILLION YEARS AGO

4.4–3.7 BILLION YEARS AGO

The **"Last Universal Common Ancestor"** (LUCA) is the earliest organism from which all modern organisms have eventually evolved. It lived sometime between the first life and the earliest fossils, but no one knows when. It's possible—but not certain—that the first living thing was also "LUCA," but it's more likely that life emerged more than once, earlier versions leaving no trace or descendants.

Free-floating cyanobacteria

3.7 BILLION YEARS AGO

Microbes called **cyanobacteria** began to photosynthesize. Cyanobacteria formed large "mats" in shallow water. Because they needed sunlight, they could only live near the surface of the water.

No one knows what LUCA looked like, but it would have been a very simple organism.

Cyanobacteria used the energy from sunlight to break down carbon dioxide and water to make a sugar called glucose and the gas oxygen. The sugar was the "fuel" the bacteria needed to run their own bodies. The oxygen was a waste product and was released. Today, all green plants photosynthesize in this way. They release the oxygen all other living things need to survive.

3.7 BILLION YEARS AGO

As sediment settled on a mat of cyanobacteria, more cyanobacteria grew on top, forming layered mounds of dead cyanobacteria and sediment that have fossilized as striped rocks called stromatolites. These are the **oldest rocks** that we can say for certain are **fossils**.

Stromatolites formed in shallow water where sunlight could reach them.

2.4–2.1 BILLION YEARS AGO

Carbon dioxide is a greenhouse gas that traps heat around Earth, keeping it warm. Cyanobacteria used up so much carbon dioxide that Earth cooled catastrophically. The planet froze, with seas and land covered in a thick layer of ice. This **"Snowball Earth"** state lasted for around 300 million years.

Snowball Earth might have had small areas of liquid water or icy slush, or it might have been entirely covered with ice.

2.1 BILLION YEARS AGO

3.4–2.4 BILLION YEARS AGO

Photosynthetic cyanobacteria **released oxygen** into the shallow seawater where they lived. At first, the oxygen was used up in chemical reactions in the oceans.

Red stripes in rock 2.2 billion years old are evidence of early oxygen.

2.4–2 BILLION YEARS AGO

Cyanobacteria were very successful. They took over areas of shallow water, forcing other microbes to live deeper in the sea. The success of cyanobacteria increased the amount of oxygen in the water where they lived until no more could stay dissolved in water. Some reacted with iron in the water, producing iron oxide (rust). Some escaped into the atmosphere. This is known as the **Great Oxygenation Event** or the "oxygen catastrophe."

2.1 BILLION–720 MILLION YEARS AGO

Scientists used to talk of the "boring billion" years—when microbes didn't do much or evolve a great deal—between around 1.8 and 0.8 billion years ago. Now it's thought that this time probably saw the first multicelled organisms, the first more complicated cells, and the first organisms to have two parents rather than one.

2.1 BILLION YEARS AGO

Below the frozen surface, volcanoes continued to erupt. They poured carbon dioxide back into the atmosphere, and Earth slowly warmed again, until the ice melted at last. The melting ice carried minerals into the ocean. These were **nutrients for the microbes** that had survived under the ice, which reproduced quickly, re-establishing life in the oceans.

2.1 BILLION YEARS AGO

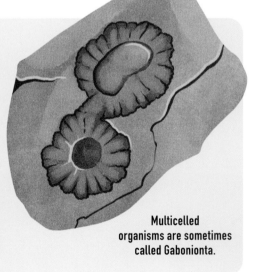

2.1 BILLION YEARS AGO

Rounded **multicelled organisms** lived in colonies on seabed that is now found in rocks in Gabon, Africa. Their fossils show that many organisms had a spherical hump in the middle and a flat, frill-like part around it, up to 17 cm (6.7 in) across. Others were shaped like tubes or strings of pearls.

Multicelled organisms are sometimes called Gabonionta.

2.1–1.8 BILLION YEARS AGO

Some microbes absorbed (but didn't digest) others. The result was larger microbes that enclosed some smaller ones that were still working inside them. Over time, they became a single organism of a type called a **eukaryote**.

BY 1.8 BILLION YEARS AGO

The first **eukaryotic cells** emerged from which all modern eukaryotes have evolved.

The arrangement of one organism living inside another is called endosymbiosis. Both organisms gain some advantage from it. The larger cell has a smaller cell working for it, producing food energy. The smaller cell has a safe environment to live in, with a supply of the chemicals it needs. Today, many simple microbes, such as bacteria, are still prokaryotes. All organisms with more than one cell, and more complex single-celled organisms, are eukaryotes.

1.56 BILLION YEARS AGO

A **multicelled organism** that was like long ribbons of seaweed lived in seas that are now part of China. Around 30 cm (1 ft) long, it could probably photosynthesize. Its cells were all much the same—it did not have different cells for different functions in its body, as more complex multicelled organisms do.

890 MILLION YEARS AGO

The first early forms of **sponges** might have appeared. Alternatively, sponges might have evolved around 780 million years ago or even later. Sponges are a simple, multicelled organism with different cell types. They filter water through a central channel, taking nutrients from it. There is no formal body structure, and a sponge that's minced up can rebuild itself into a working sponge!

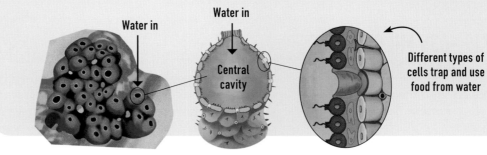

Water in

Water in

Central cavity

Different types of cells trap and use food from water

1.25 BILLION YEARS AGO

The first **simple plants** probably evolved in the oceans.

1—0.9 BILLION YEARS AGO

The earliest known type of **fungus** lived in the region that is now Canada.

720 MILLION YEARS AGO

800—700 MILLION YEARS AGO

Amoeba, red algae, and **foraminfera** became widespread in the sea. Foraminifera are simple single-celled organisms that make a chalky shell around themselves.

Asexual reproduction produces a clone, an exact copy of the parent. This is easy and enables a single organism to start colonizing a new area. It works well if conditions don't change. Sexual reproduction allows mixing of characteristics between generations, producing varied organisms. Variety is a good protection against changes in the environment and allows organisms to evolve quickly to suit new conditions.

Bangiomorpha, about 0.025 mm (0.001 in) across

1.07 BILLION YEARS AGO

Bangiomorpha, a type of red algae, is the earliest known organism to **reproduce sexually**. This means that cells from two parents are needed to make a new organism. Previously, an organism split in half, making a copy of itself, to reproduce asexually.

720 MILLION YEARS AGO

Earth was again plunged into **snowball conditions**—at least twice, possibly three times—putting life on hold again.

719–556 MILLION YEARS AGO

As Earth emerged from the freezer, strange organisms flourished. These all had soft bodies that don't fossilize easily, so the 200 known types are probably a tiny fraction of those that lived. The earliest were neither plants nor animals, but the first animals (except perhaps sponges) appeared later in this period.

Bragdatia was a lettuce-like rangeomorph, 50 cm (1 ft 8in) across.

Charnia, a fernlike rangeomorph, was usually small, but some grew to nearly 2 m (6.5 ft) tall.

719–635 MILLION YEARS AGO

Ice covered the planet's surface for tens of millions of years. It might have been a "slushball" rather than a snowball event, with areas remaining unfrozen.

570–556 MILLION YEARS AGO

The first large organisms were **rangeomorphs,** which had soft, quilted bodies. Stuck to the seabed, they absorbed microbes and nutrients from the water. They had a fractal body plan, built from shapes repeated at a decreasing scale, like the fronds of a fern. Rangeomorphs didn't have different body parts for different functions. They dominated the seas for nearly 20 million years.

719 MILLION YEARS AGO

635 MILLION YEARS AGO

Carbon dioxide built up enough to melt the ice. Meltwater carried **minerals from rocks into the sea**, boosting growth of photosynthesizing cyanobacteria and algae.

575–565 MILLION YEARS AGO

Thectardis was a cone-shaped organism that **filtered food** from the water flowing around it.

Thectardis, 15 cm (5.9 in) tall

567–550 MILLION YEARS AGO

Dickinsonia is one of the **earliest known animals**. It fed on the microbial mat (see page 21) and could probably move around—its possible fossilized trails have been found. It grew to 1.4 m (4.6 ft) across, but was only a few millimeters (a fraction of an inch) thick.

Dickinsonia grew new segments from the front, making the animal larger.

565 MILLION YEARS AGO

The first **flatworms** appeared, the first organism to have sense organs at the head end. They had simple, undivided bodies with two matching halves. Now, most animals have this type of body, called a **bilateral body plan**.

560 MILLION YEARS AGO

Haootia is the earliest known **animal with muscles**. An ancestor of jellyfish, it was fixed to the seabed and waved its arms in the current.

558—555 MILLION YEARS AGO

Parvancorina lay on the seabed, lined up with currents to feed efficiently. It was possibly an **ancestor of arthropods**, animals with hard, jointed outsides such as centipedes, insects, and crabs.

Parvancorina,
1–3 cm (0.4–1.2 in)

556 MILLION YEARS AGO

Tribrachidium,
4 cm (1.6 in) across

558—555 MILLION YEARS AGO

Tribrachidium lived fixed to the seabed. It had **three-part radial symmetry**, meaning that its shape was made by rotating one part around a midpoint, copying it to make three identical sections. Modern starfish and sea urchins also have radial symmetry, with five or more identical parts.

Animals that could move had a huge advantage over those fixed in one place. They could leave overcrowded places, move toward more food, or away from danger. At first, there wasn't much danger. But when animals began to feed on each other, being able to hide—or hunt—became important to survival.

558—555 MILLION YEARS AGO

Kimberella could move on a **single muscular foot** like a snail as it searched for scraps of food. Its head was at the end of a flexible, extendable arm. It had a tough shell on its back, topped with hard scales.

Kimberella, up to 10 cm (4 in)

555–535 MILLION YEARS AGO

Once animals began to move around, change came more quickly. Some began to burrow into the seabed or swam through the sea. Sexual reproduction, first seen in algae, now began to appear in animals.

555 MILLION YEARS AGO

Spriggina is the first animal considered to have a **head and its sensory organs mostly at the front**. It had a segmented body. This type of body can easily evolve into a more complex organism, since it can grow by adding more segments, and functional features can be added to some segments (such as claws or legs).

Spriggina, 3–5 cm (1.2–2 in) long, was a soft creature with up to 40 segments.

555 MILLION YEARS AGO

555 MILLION YEARS AGO

An early **bilateral animal**, *Ikaria* was a soft-bodied, bean-shaped creature half the size of a grain of rice.

550 MILLION YEARS AGO

Cloudina was possibly a type of worm or cnidarian. It built a series of conical funnel-shaped shells, forming a hard tube that it lived inside. It's the earliest example of an animal with a **simple gut** and one of the earliest with a shell. The shell probably protected it against some of the first predators.

555 MILLION YEARS AGO

Funisia is one of the first known animals to **reproduce sexually**. It was anchored to the seabed, grew in large colonies, and released its eggs and sperm into the current. It could probably also reproduce by budding, like sponges and coral. It might have been related to sponges or cnidarians (animals like jellyfish).

Funisia, 30 cm (1 ft) tall, waved its flexible, wormlike body in the water, trapping food.

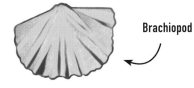

Brachiopod

550 MILLION YEARS AGO

The **first brachiopods** appeared. These are shellfish with two hinged halves of shell, like modern mussels and clams. The shell opens, and the animal filters food from seawater flowing through it.

550 MILLION YEARS AGO

Tiny, branching **seaweeds** appeared in seas that are now in China and Brazil.

549–542 MILLION YEARS AGO

Namacalathus was a very early **shell-forming organism**, one of the first to attach above the seabed in reef-like structures.

543 MILLION YEARS AGO

With one end of a thick, tubular outside stuck in the seabed, colonies of *Corumbella* **fed on particles in the water** that streamed past them.

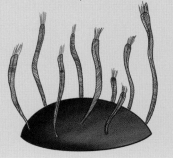

535 MILLION YEARS AGO

542–532 MILLION YEARS AGO

Everything lived either on or just below a seabed covered by a **microbial mat**, often several centimeters (an inch or two) thick. Tiny animals began to burrow into the mud and sand below, mixing the layers. This brought oxygen into the mud, killing microbes that couldn't tolerate oxygen. Soon, larger animals began to burrow and penetrate farther, changing the seabed.

Microbial mat

Animal grazing on mat

Before the Cambrian, everything lived on top of the seabed or just below the surface.

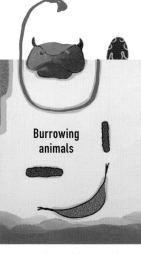

Burrowing animals

Later, animals burrowed into the seabed.

Small, shelly fossils from this time show that animals were beginning to develop a hard, protective outside. They did this by absorbing minerals such as calcium carbonate from seawater. Most small, shelly fossils are parts of small organisms, such as scales, spines, and fragments of shell. Arthropods such as insects, crabs, and scorpions still have mineralized external skeletons.

535 MILLION YEARS AGO

Halkieria, an early type of **mollusk** (like slugs and snails), had a shell cap at each end and was covered with 2,000 tiny protective plates—just the kind of piece that could become a small, shelly fossil.

534–501 MILLION YEARS AGO

It was cold at the end of the Ediacaran, 541 million years ago, but as it warmed, life blossomed, exploding into new forms. Previously almost everything had lived on the seabed, moving only slowly and feeding on tiny particles floating in the current, but now life became more active. Animals became better at hunting or protecting themselves from being eaten, their bodies changing in a race for survival.

534–520 MILLION YEARS AGO

The **"Cambrian Explosion"** is the name given to a huge increase in the variety of organisms that occurred in the Cambrian (542–488.3 million years ago).

530 MILLION YEARS AGO

The first **trilobites** appeared. They became some of the **most successful animals of all time**, surviving in different forms for over 250 million years. Around 80–90 percent of fossils from the Cambrian seabed are trilobites.

Like other trilobites, *Olenellus* could see well.

534 MILLION YEARS AGO

530–520 MILLION YEARS AGO

Archaeocyathids were some of the **first reef-building animals**. Cup-shaped early sponges, they filtered food from the shallow tropical seas where they lived.

525–518 MILLION YEARS AGO

The area of Chengjiang in China, a shallow sea at the time, was home to many **soft-bodied animals**. Unusual conditions in Chengjiang led to them being fossilized, revealing astonishing details about some of the earliest complicated life forms.

520 MILLION YEARS AGO

Tiny arthropod *Kummingella* was one of the **first animals to look after its eggs**. The female carried up to 80 eggs, protected under the edge of her shell. *Fuixanhuia* went further, **looking after her young**—an adult was found with four tiny young alongside her.

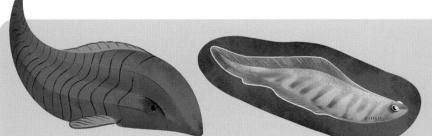

Myllokunmingia was one of the first animals to have a skull, though not yet made of bone.

Haikuoichthys had at least six gills.

518 MILLION YEARS AGO

Early **fishlike animals** appeared, with a simple dorsal fin along the back and gills to breathe. These were probably **very early chordates**—animals with a stiff, gristly rod in the back that was a step toward having a backbone. All were small, around 2.5 cm (1 in) long.

518—499 MILLION YEARS AGO

Anomalocaris was the **first large predator** of its time. An arthropod, it had compound eyes, but no legs, moving through the water by wafting its flaps up and down.

Anomalocaris, 37 cm (15 in) long

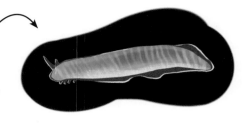

Pikaia was a leaf-shaped animal with short tentacles near the mouth.

513—505 MILLION YEARS AGO

Pikaia was a strange animal that **doesn't quite fit into any category**. It was a little like a worm, a bit like a fish, a bit like an arthropod—but not actually any of these. It probably had gill slits but also a hard covering called a cuticle, like the outside of an insect. Scientists can't even decide whether it was a vertebrate or an invertebrate. With a flattened body, it swam by wriggling, making a zigzag shape through the water.

510 MILLION YEARS AGO

The oldest **trace fossils** found on land suggest a sluglike animal, and some early arthropods began to venture from the sea.

501 MILLION YEARS AGO

Aysheaia, 2.5—5 cm (1—2 in) long, was very much like the modern land-going velvet worm and probably an ancestor of one of the first animals to move onto land.

Marrella, 2.5 cm (1 in) long, was one of the most common creatures in the Burgess Shale. It scuttled and swam using its many legs.

508 MILLION YEARS AGO

The **Burgess Shale**, in Canada, is a vast fossil bed created from a Cambrian seafloor. Like Chengjiang, it contains very well-preserved animals in huge numbers.

Hallucigenia, up to 5 cm (2 in) long, was a soft, tube-shaped animal with short legs and spines along the back. Varieties have been found in both China and the Burgess Shale.

Odontogriphus, 6 cm (2.4 in) long, had a round mouth packed with teeth, possibly an early version of the radula (grating mouth) of modern mollusks.

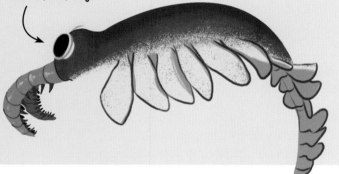

ANIMALS FOR THE FUTURE

The Cambrian Explosion saw huge changes in the bodies and lifestyles of animals, setting up the pattern for the animals alive now. The evidence of the "explosion" comes from fossils left less than 520 million years ago, mostly in China and Canada. There must have been many "ghost" groups of in-between forms earlier that have not fossilized.

LIFE GETS TOUGH

In the period from 540–520 million years ago, life changed radically. From stationary lives on or just below the seabed, feeding on what fell their way through the water, animals changed to **moving around, eating each other,** and actively **hunting and escaping** one another.

ARMS RACE

When an animal is not in danger of being eaten, it can have a soft body and lie on the seabed safely. But if there are predators keen to feed on it, it needs **protection**. Animals began to grow shells in the late Ediacaran, and by the middle of the Cambrian they had developed a variety of spikes, hard scales, teeth, and claws. These evolved quickly, as predators and prey raced against each other to become well equipped. If a prey animal developed a hard outside, a predator needed sharp teeth, strong jaws, or crushing pincers to break through and eat it. Those that had no hard outside of their own might bury themselves underground or hide between the rocks and hard parts of a reef. The worm *Eximipriapulus* lived like a modern hermit crab, moving into the empty shell of a hyolith, a long, tube-shaped shellfish.

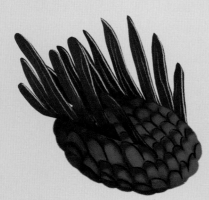

Wiwaxia, up to 5 cm (2 in) long, was a mollusk that lived 520–505 million years ago. Scales and spines protected it from predators.

Helicocystis, 0.5–2 cm (0.1–0.8 in) long, was an ancestor of starfish. Spiral grooves around its hard body opened and closed to catch food.

Sidneyia, 5–12.7 cm (2–5 in) long, walked along the seabed eating other hard-shelled animals.

EYES SPY

The Cambrian saw the first animals with **eyes**, although some earlier organisms could detect light and shade. Eyes allowed animals to see others they could eat, or that might eat them, and so move toward or away from them. Trilobites perhaps had the best eyes. Like the compound eyes of modern insects, they had thousands of separate tiny lenses that, when put together, made a mosaic image of the world around them. Eyes are so useful to animals that they have evolved separately many times.

Opabinia made the most of the development of eyes, growing five! Up to 7 cm (3 in) long, it lived on the seabed, using its long, clawed proboscis to snatch food and pass it to its mouth.

At 50 cm (1.6 ft) long, *Titanokorys* was one of the largest animals of its time.

MARCHING TOWARD THE FUTURE

Many of the features of modern animals appeared first in the Cambrian. Modern vertebrates (animals with backbones) have all evolved from those with a **notochord**—a stiff rod running along the body—in the Cambrian seas.

Modern arthropods, including insects, spiders, scorpions, crabs, and prawns, have all developed from the animals with hard, jointed outsides and segmented bodies. Echinoderms such as starfish and sea urchins have developed from Cambrian ancestors like *Helicocystis*. Annelid worms (worms with bodies divided into ring-like segments), cnidarians like jellyfish and anemones, and mollusks such as slugs and snails all started out in the Cambrian.

The notochord became the backbone in later animals.

CHAPTER 2

THE MOVE TO LAND

Until half a billion years ago, all living things on Earth were in the sea. Then, some organisms moved onto land. Within 100 million years, huge forests blanketed the land.

While all life was in the oceans, the arrangement of Earth's land was of little importance to living things. There were shallow seas around the margins of the land, which were warmer or cooler depending on where they lay, but conditions on land didn't matter. Once organisms colonized land, the movement of the landmasses and the climate on land became more important. Earth has seen times when almost all land was clustered in one giant supercontinent and times when—as now—it is spread between several clumps. It has seen periods of heat and cold. Weather is affected by the arrangement of land, with huge continents often having a dry interior and rain falling over mountains near the coast. All this affected life as it spread inward from the shores.

500—445 MILLION YEARS AGO

The end of the Cambrian and the following period, the Ordovician, were warm. The average air temperature was nearly 50° C (120° F) and the sea temperature near the equator was as warm as bathwater, at 43° C (110° F). The move to land probably began with algae and plants covering rocks in tidal areas. Animals followed, eating the plants or perhaps escaping briefly from the perils of the sea to a place predators couldn't follow.

500 MILLION YEARS AGO

Microbial mats (thin layers of microorganisms) grew on tidal flats and beaches, starting to make the **first soil**. The first land plants might have appeared, too. Methods of calculating evolution from looking at DNA suggests they arrived this early, but no fossils have been found.

488 MILLION YEARS AGO

An **extinction event** (see pages 30–31) seems to have wiped out many organisms in the late Cambrian. It might have been caused by colder weather, less oxygen in the seas, or perhaps volcanic eruptions. After it, new organisms soon appeared in the **Great Ordovician Biodiversity Event** (GOBE).

485—460 MILLION YEARS AGO

The first reef-forming **corals** appeared.

500 MILLION YEARS AGO

488—443 MILLION YEARS AGO

The GOBE saw a fourfold increase in the number of different marine organisms. Lots of **phytoplankton** (tiny organisms that photosynthesize) bloomed in the sea, providing food for other organisms. The result was the first coral reefs, the first bivalves (hinged, two-part shells), gastropods (like snails), bryozoans ("moss animals") and crinoids (or "sea lilies").

475 MILLION YEARS AGO

The first firm evidence of plants on land is the fossilized spore of a **liverwort** (a simple plant).

Arandapsis, 15 cm (6 in) long, was one of the first jawless fish.

Another armored jawless fish, *Astraspis*, lived 468–450 million years ago.

480—470 MILLION YEARS AGO

Arandaspis was an early **jawless fish** and one of the first known true **vertebrates**. The only jawless fish today are lampreys and hagfish. *Arandaspis* probably filtered food from seawater. The front of the animal was covered with knobbly armored plates, with gaps for its eyes and gills. It had bony strips of armor behind, extending to the tail. Armored jawless fish became common in the Ordovician seas.

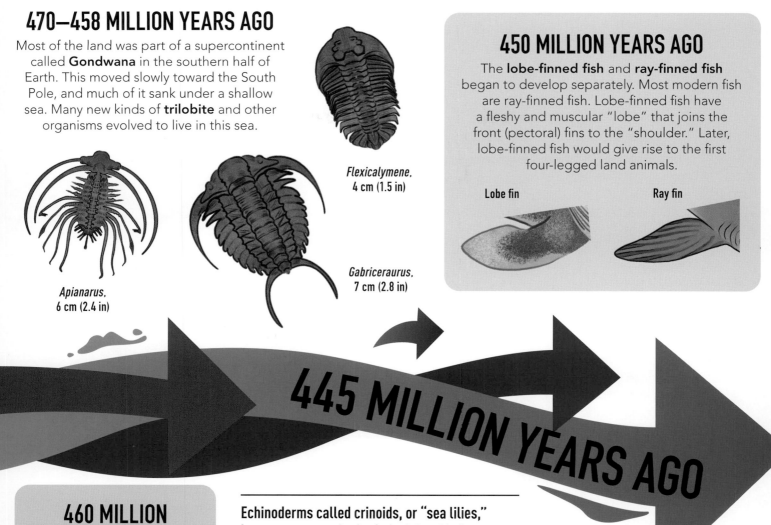

470–458 MILLION YEARS AGO

Most of the land was part of a supercontinent called **Gondwana** in the southern half of Earth. This moved slowly toward the South Pole, and much of it sank under a shallow sea. Many new kinds of **trilobite** and other organisms evolved to live in this sea.

Flexicalymene,
4 cm (1.5 in)

Gabriceraurus,
7 cm (2.8 in)

Apianarus,
6 cm (2.4 in)

450 MILLION YEARS AGO

The **lobe-finned fish** and **ray-finned fish** began to develop separately. Most modern fish are ray-finned fish. Lobe-finned fish have a fleshy and muscular "lobe" that joins the front (pectoral) fins to the "shoulder." Later, lobe-finned fish would give rise to the first four-legged land animals.

Lobe fin

Ray fin

445 MILLION YEARS AGO

460 MILLION YEARS AGO

Plants appeared on land. First, green algae moved onto the shore and then evolved into simple plants—**moss, liverworts,** and **lichens**. To begin with, plants only grew around the coast and along the paths of rivers.

Moss is found even today covering surfaces in damp places.

Echinoderms called crinoids, or "sea lilies," became common in the Ordovician. Modern echinoderms are animals such as starfish, brittle stars, and sea urchins. They have a hard outside and radial symmetry (their body shape is made by rotating one part around a middle point). Crinoids were fixed to the seabed by a stalk, the arms wafting in the water to catch food.

Crinoids looked like plants but were animals.

The crinoid *Glyptocrinus* had up to 20 "branches" above its cup.

445 MILLION YEARS AGO

The **end-Ordovician extinction event** killed 85 percent of all species of organisms in two bursts, about a million years apart.

29

CATASTROPHE!

At the end of the Ordovician, most of the species (types) of organism living on Earth died out. In total, 85 percent of species died. An event that kills more than 75 percent of species over a relatively short period (in geological terms) is called a "mass extinction event." There have been five major extinction events since multicelled life evolved.

DANGER SIGNS

Mass extinctions have many causes, but all involve **changes to the climate** (the patterns of weather and temperature). The climate can be changed by how landmasses move around, by the activity of organisms, and by catastrophic events such as massive volcanic eruptions—and even a large asteroid crashing into Earth. We don't know the exact causes of some mass extinction events.

BLAME THE PLANTS?

The extinction event at the end of the Ordovician was possibly caused by **volcanic eruptions** heating the planet—but scientists once thought it was produced by cooling and widespread ice. Whatever the cause, 85 percent of species died out.

An extinction event 375 million years ago might have been caused by **plants**. It happened as land plants spread around the world. Perhaps plants removed so much carbon dioxide from the atmosphere that temperatures dropped. A second wave of extinctions followed, maybe caused by volcanic eruptions or even falling meteors.

WORST OF ALL

The most devastating mass extinction of all has been called the **"Great Dying."** At the end of the Permian period, 252 million years ago, around 95 percent of all species died out. Huge volcanic eruptions flooded all of Siberia in northern Russia with lava, resulting in disastrous **climate change**.

END OF THE DINOSAURS

The non-bird dinosaurs (see pages 80-81) died in an extinction event 65.5 million years ago, caused by a huge **asteroid** crashing into Earth.

IT'S NOT OVER YET

Scientists believe a **sixth extinction event** is happening right now. The cause this time is human activity. We have caused problematic climate change by burning a lot of fossil fuels (gas, oil, and coal), which adds carbon dioxide to the atmosphere and causes the planet to heat. In addition, we have destroyed many of the environments that organisms need to live in, hunted some species to extinction, and upset the balance of organisms. It's impossible to tell yet how devastating this extinction event will be or which organisms will survive it.

LEFT BEHIND

Not everything dies in a mass extinction. **Ecosystems rebuild** from the organisms that survive the disaster. The extinction frees up some niches (specialized living spaces), allowing space and resources for survivors to spread out and flourish with little competition. The surviving organisms evolve to suit the new conditions in the spaces they live, and species diversify again. Often, there is a period of quick diversification once conditions have settled after a mass extinction.

Tardigrades, or "water bears," are tiny organisms a few millimeters (a fraction of an inch) long. They have surived all five mass extinctions.

444—420 MILLION YEARS AGO

Within a few million years, life recovered from the mass extinction event at the end of the Ordovician. The new period, called the Silurian, saw dramatic changes, the most important being the spread of animals from the sea to the land. There remained a lot of sea to live in: Sea levels near the start of the period were 100—200 m (328—656 ft) higher than they are now.

Dolicophonus, 2.5 cm (1 in) long, was a scorpion that probably spent time both in the sea and on land.

As plants grew, they added oxygen to the atmosphere. Once there was enough oxygen in the air, some of it began to change to a different form called ozone, which used energy from sunlight. The ozone made a layer near the top of the atmosphere that blocked the damaging ultraviolet radiation in sunlight. Water also blocks this radiation, so life in the sea was always possible, but the land was dangerous. Finally, with the radiation blocked, organisms could safely leave the sea and live on land.

437.5—436.5 MILLION YEARS AGO

Scorpions were some of the **earliest animals to leave the sea** and make trips onto land, finally becoming fully land-based.

444 MILLION YEARS AGO

Conodont animals like *Promissum* became much more common. Conodonts were early vertebrates and were probably the **first vertebrates to have teeth**. They lived from around 500 to 200 million years ago. Usually, the teeth are the only parts of these animals preserved as fossils, but *Promissum*'s body has also been fossilized, showing that it looked like a worm or eel. It kept moving all the time, as modern sharks do.

Promissum, 30 cm (12 in) long

438—433 MILLION YEARS AGO

The ancestors of modern sharks and rays are sometimes called **"spiny sharks."** They had a shark-like shape, a skeleton of cartilage instead of bone, and a spine at the base of each fin.

433 MILLION YEARS AGO

The **first vascular plant** to appear was a type of *Cooksonia*. Vascular plants have special tissue that forms channels or ducts to move water around the plant. *Cooksonia*'s roots spread over the rocks rather than underground, and it grew near sources of water. It had short stems just a few centimeters (or inches) tall and no leaves. Stems ended with a sporangium, a capsule that produced spores for the plant to reproduce.

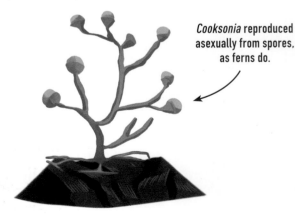

Cooksonia reproduced asexually from spores, as ferns do.

THE MOVE TO LAND

432–418 MILLION YEARS AGO

Eurypterus was a **giant sea scorpion** that could venture onto land. Its last pair of legs grew large, adapted for use as paddles when swimming. Legs farther forward could be used for crawling over the seabed. They were covered in spines that *Eurypterus* probably used to hold prey while breaking it up with its pincers. *Eurypterus* spent most of its time in the sea, but could crawl over the coast to spawn (lay eggs) in water.

Eurypterus grew up to 1.3 m (4.3 ft) long.

The first animals to evolve especially to live on land were arthropods such as millipedes. Millipedes today are little changed from these first pioneers. There are 12,000 named species alive now. Although the first millipedes were small, some later grew to 2 m (7 ft) long. Today, the largest are 38 cm (15 in) long.

428 MILLION YEARS AGO

One of the earliest known land animals, *Cowiedesmus* was a type of **millipede**, 4 cm (1.5 in) long, that lived in the area that is now Scotland.

420 MILLION YEARS AGO

Prototaxites

430–350 MILLION YEARS AGO

Giant **columns of fungus** called Prototaxites towered over the Silurian landscape, one of the strangest organisms of all time. Long before there were large plants on land, these unbranched columns grew to 8 m (26 ft) tall. A few scientists think instead that the fossils of Protaxites might be rolled-up mats of simple, small plants like liverwort. They remain a mystery.

Baragwanathia grew roots from stems that bent over on the ground.

422–393 MILLION YEARS AGO

The **first large land plant**, *Baragwanathia*, grew branching stems up to 1 m (3.3 ft) long, covered with small, needle-like leaves. It sprawled over marshy ground, sending upright branches from the trailing stems. The earliest types of *Baragwanathia* grew in areas that were covered by seawater at high tide but exposed to the air at low tide. Later types lived entirely on land.

419–390 MILLION YEARS AGO

The period from 419 to 359 million years ago is the Devonian, known as the "age of fish." It was a warm time, with high sea levels and a tropical sea temperature of around 30° C (86° F). But the Devonian didn't just see a huge increase in the types of fish. It also saw life thoroughly established on land—more than four billion years after the planet formed.

419–416 MILLION YEARS AGO

The first known **ray-finned fish** appeared, called *Andreolepis*.

416–398 MILLION YEARS AGO

Armored fish began to take over the seas. With bony armor plates covering their bodies, they were well protected against predators. But bony plates make a fish less flexible. *Pteraspis* solved the problem by having plates at the front and smaller bony scales at the back. Bony projections gave it stability and streamlining in the water, since it had no fins.

Pteraspis,
20 cm (8 in) long

419 MILLION YEARS AGO

Entelognathus,
20 cm (7.8 in) long

414 MILLION YEARS AGO

The millipede *Pneumodesmus* was one of the earliest known arthropods to have **spiracles**—small holes in the side of the body through which it breathed. Spiracles are only useful for breathing on land.

419 MILLION YEARS AGO

The first **fish with modern jaws** was the placoderm (armored fish) *Entelognathus*. With two jaws joined with a hinge, *Entelognathus* could open and close its mouth to take bites. Nothing had been able to bite in this way before. Earlier placoderms had a simple, beaklike jaw. The first land-going vertebrates would have jaws like *Entelognathus*.

Rhyniella,
just 1.5 mm (a fraction of an inch) long

412–391 MILLION YEARS AGO

The **first insects** were animals like *Rhyniella*, a little like a modern springtail. These tiny creatures would have crawled through the moss, lichen, and early plants on land.

410 MILLION YEARS AGO

Palaeocharinus was an early **arachnid** (the same type of animal as spiders). It lived on land. Although it looks like a spider, it didn't spin a web.

Palaeocharinus,
0.5 cm (0.2 in)

400 MILLION YEARS AGO

Nautilids were **cephalopods**—animals like squids—that grew a hard, protective shell. Nautilids had appeared in the Ordovician with long, straight, cone-shaped shells, but during the Devonian the shells began first to curve and then to curl. These are called ammonoids. Later, they evolved into ammonites with their characteristic spiral shells, which swam in the Jurassic seas 200 million years later.

Ammonite

Nautilid

390 MILLION YEARS AGO

407 MILLION YEARS AGO

The first known **freshwater amoeba** lived in Scotland in small pools.

Only the skull of
Euporosteus survives.

392–375 MILLION YEARS AGO

The lobe-finned fish *Eusthenopteron* grew **strong pectoral fins**. Although it probably stayed in the water itself, these sturdy, prop-like fins were a vital stage on the path to walking on land.

411–407 MILLION YEARS AGO

Euporosteus is the oldest type of **coelacanth**, a lobe-finned fish that still survives today. Coelocanths were once thought to have become extinct 65.5 million years ago, but some were found still living in 1938.

Eusthenopteron, 1.8 m (6 ft) long

FROM ROCK TO FOREST

The transformation of Earth's land from barren rock to teeming forests took less than 100 million years, but it began with something that sounds very dull: the creation of soil. For large plants and trees to survive on the ground, they needed to have roots anchored in soil. Plants both make and need soil—they developed together.

SUPER SOIL

We don't pay much attention to **soil**, but it's vital to life on land. Made of tiny bits of rock and a lot of organic (life-based) material, it provides plants with nutrients, water, and a way of staying stable by holding their roots in place. The organic matter is a mix of bacteria, fungi, and other microorganisms, along with dead plant and animal matter that they are breaking down. Soil has lots of gaps. These can hold water, which plants take as they need it.

FIRST SOILS

The first organisms to grow on land were **algae, lichen,** and various **microorganisms**. When these died, their tiny bodies were added to the early soil. Weathering by wind and water, and even the action of organisms growing over the surface, wore away tiny fragments of rock that collected in the soil. Plants and the microbes that lived around them produced chemical weathering, making acids and other chemicals that helped break down rocks.

Without soil, early plants sprawled over the ground (mid-Silurian). As the first organic soil collected, plants were able to put down deeper roots (early Devonian), and finally even trees could become firmly anchored (late Devonian).

425 million years ago

410 million years ago

370 million years ago

FIRST PLANTS, FIRST BUGS

The first plants to grow were low to the ground with no roots or leaves. They didn't need much soil to live. The very first plants—**lichens**—could even live on completely bare rock, which they helped to weather. The plants provided cover and food for microbes and small arthropods that left the water to live on land. Soil collected from decaying parts of the first plants and animals, and soon larger plants could survive and support larger animals. By the middle of the Devonian, 390 million years ago, larger plants with both leaves and roots covered the landscape. There were forests of plants the size of shrubs, including **ferns, horsetails,** and **lycophytes** (fernlike plants), and even the first **trees.**

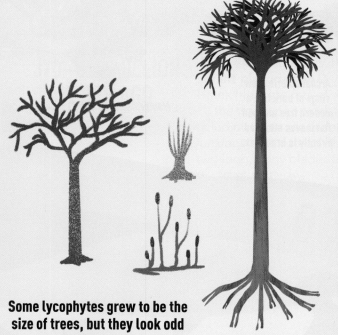

Some lycophytes grew to be the size of trees, but they look odd compared with modern trees.

The same plant at different stages of growth

Bare trunk   Leaves on trunk   Branches with leaves

TALL AS TREES

Some of the **fernlike trees** grew as tall as modern trees. *Eospermatopteris* was the earliest known treelike plant. It grew to be 8 m (26 ft) tall and 1 m (3.3 ft) across. Unlike most modern trees, though, it had a thick bulbous base, a long trunk with branches only at the top, and a relatively small, thin canopy of leafless branches above. Its center of gravity was low, so that it did not easily blow over. This was important because its roots were still shallow.

359–315 MILLION YEARS AGO

When trees returned after the extinction event 359 million years ago, they took over. Hot, humid forests sprang up around the planet. The huge increase in large land plants led to more oxygen in the atmosphere than at any other time in Earth's history.

Medullosa

Sigillaria

359–300 MILLION YEARS AGO

Giant **clubmoss trees**, such as *Sigillaria*, dominated the forests. They had long trunks with a honeycomb pattern of scales, the scars left where a single, grasslike leaf had grown. Lower leaves fell off, so the tree only ever had leaves at the top. Its cones grew directly from the trunk, just under the crown. *Lepidodendron* was a type of tree known as a **scale tree** that could grow to 50 m (160 ft) tall and 2 m (6.6 ft) across the base. It had little woody tissue compared to modern trees; instead its bark gave it the strength to withstand winds. *Medullosa* was another common type of tree, a **seed fern**. It grew huge, fernlike leaves divided into smaller leaflets. *Medullosa* grew heavy seeds as large as eggs and large pollen organs that held unusually large pollen. They were possibly pollinated by animals of some kind.

359 MILLION YEARS AGO

350–340 MILLION YEARS AGO

The first insects to evolve **wings** began flying over the swamps of the Carboniferous.

Oxygen levels drove both the evolution of insects and forest fires. Fire needs oxygen to burn, and the more oxygen there is, the more easily fires start and spread. With high levels of oxygen and plenty of wood, forest fires became common. More oxygen also meant that insects could grow much larger than they do today. Insects don't actively breathe, but absorb oxygen from air that flows passively into holes along their sides called "spiracles."

345–200 MILLION YEARS AGO

The **largest land-going arthropod** of all time was *Arthropleura*, a millipede that grew to 2.5 m (8.6 ft) long. It probably ate plant matter, as modern millipedes generally do.

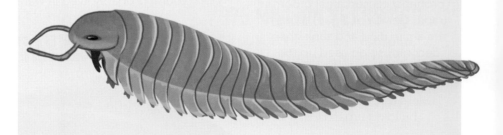

A trail of footprints left by *Arthropleura* has been fossilized in Scotland.

Pulmonoscorpius,
70 cm (27.5 in)

336—326 MILLION YEARS AGO

A **giant scorpion**, *Pulmonoscorpius*, probably fed on small amphibians, early reptiles, and smaller arthropods.

331—323 MILLION YEARS AGO

The predatory *Proterogyrinus* was one of the first amphibians to have long, curved ribs and muscles that could move them to pump air in and out of its lungs for **breathing on land**. It walked with a wriggling gait, and its name means "early wriggler." It ate fish that it caught from the rivers and pools.

Proterogyrinus,
2.5 m (8 ft)

330 MILLION YEARS AGO

The **first early amphibian**, *Balanerpton*, appeared. It was among the first tetrapods fully adapted to life on land, only returning to the water to breed.

315 MILLION YEARS AGO

330—300 MILLION YEARS AGO

The **largest-ever freshwater fish**, *Rhizodus*, lived in rivers and swamps feeding on amphibians. With fang-like teeth up to 22 cm (9 in) long, it was a top predator that could even eat small sharks.

Rhizodus, 6 m
(19.5 ft) long

316—309 MILLION YEARS AGO

Many fossils of the **early amphibian** *Dendrerpeton* have been found inside fossilized tree trunks. Perhaps they hid or became trapped there during forest fires.

Dendrerpeton, 35 cm
(1.2 ft) long

FROM TREES TO COAL

The trees of the Carboniferous swamps have become the coal that we now burn, more than 300 million years after the trees died. As we burn it, we release carbon dioxide made with carbon that has been locked away ever since.

FOSSILIZED WOOD

When trees began to grow all around the world, their **wood** was a new kind of material. Trees first developed **bark** around 360 million years ago, when the microorganisms such as bacteria and fungi that now make wood decompose had not yet evolved. The swamps were environments with little oxygen under the water, so even soft plants such as ferns could not easily decompose.

Between the clubmoss trees, tree ferns, giant horsetails, and conifers, ferns covered the ground of the last Carboniferous, with vines and climbing plants threaded through the trees.

MAKING COAL

The plants of the swamps lived their lives and died, falling to the ground and into the water, and being replaced by new plants. Over a long time, the dead vegetation built up. Some of it could decay, but much could not. As more continued to pile up, that buried deepest was squashed. The pressure and temperature increased, and eventually the plant matter underwent chemical changes in these conditions, to become coal. Much of the oxygen, water, and nitrogen escaped, leaving **carbon**, which is the main ingredient of coal. The higher the carbon content, the better the quality of coal.

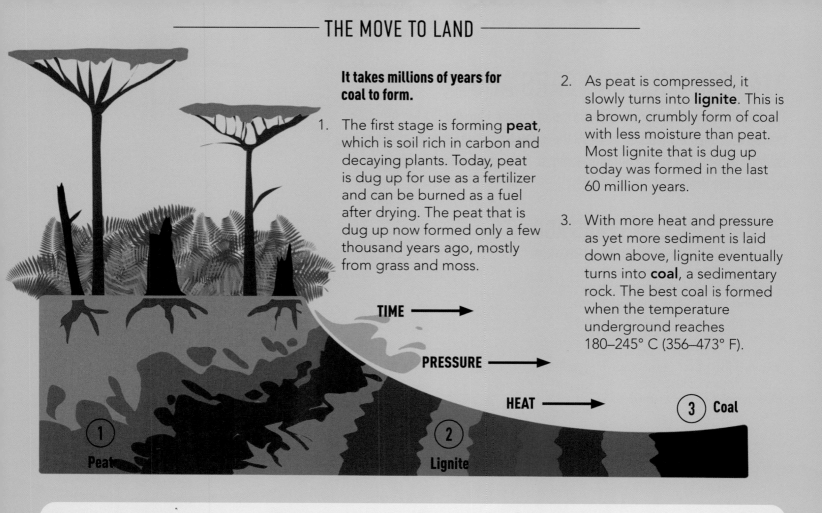

It takes millions of years for coal to form.

1. The first stage is forming **peat**, which is soil rich in carbon and decaying plants. Today, peat is dug up for use as a fertilizer and can be burned as a fuel after drying. The peat that is dug up now formed only a few thousand years ago, mostly from grass and moss.

2. As peat is compressed, it slowly turns into **lignite**. This is a brown, crumbly form of coal with less moisture than peat. Most lignite that is dug up today was formed in the last 60 million years.

3. With more heat and pressure as yet more sediment is laid down above, lignite eventually turns into **coal**, a sedimentary rock. The best coal is formed when the temperature underground reaches 180–245° C (356–473° F).

TIME ➡

PRESSURE ➡

HEAT ➡

① Peat

② Lignite

③ Coal

DUG UP

About 90 percent of the coal that we use now was laid down in the **Carboniferous** (359–299 million years ago) and the **Permian**, the period immediately after it, although some is more recent. Although it needs high temperatures underground, much of the Carboniferous coal formed during a cold period when there was widespread ice. The temperature below ground is raised by pressure and by the hot magma within Earth.

Coal-burning power plant

PUTTING BACK THE CARBON

When we burn coal to heat our homes or to make electricity, the carbon in the coal combines with oxygen from the atmosphere to make **carbon dioxide**. That carbon was originally taken from the atmosphere by the plants living 300–350 million years ago and has been locked away since they died. When plants removed carbon from the atmosphere it caused cold conditions. Burning the coal now releases carbon dioxide, which is heating the world today at a dangerous rate.

314–300 MILLION YEARS AGO

The huge forests took carbon dioxide out of the air, causing the temperature to drop and big ice sheets to form. At the same time, two large continents collided to form the supercontinent Pangea, forcing up mountain ranges, including the Urals and Apalachians.

Phlegethontia, 70–100 cm (2.3–3.3 ft) long, had a pointed snout with lots of sharp teeth.

313–307 MILLION YEARS AGO

Also called the **"scissor-toothed shark,"** *Edestus* had jaws like shears. A modern shark's worn teeth drop out and are replaced by new teeth moving forward, but *Edestus* instead grew teeth embedded in new gum at the back of the mouth. This pushed the older gums and teeth forward, and the mouth grew larger as the shark aged.

Edestus, possibly 6 m (20 ft) long

310 MILLION YEARS AGO

Eogyrinus was an amphibian that looked something like a cross between a tadpole and a crocodile, growing up to 4.5 m (15 ft). It fed on fish, its tiny legs adapted to weaving through swamp water clogged with dense plants and roots. Just a little later, *Phlegethontia* took reduced legs even further. Looking like a snake with a long, flexible body, it was an **amphibian that had lost its legs**.

314 MILLION YEARS AGO

312 MILLION YEARS AGO

The **first reptiles** appeared. They differed from amphibians in living all their life on land and laying their eggs there. The first reptiles were small, but later the dinosaurs grew to be the largest animals ever to walk the land.

Paleothyris, just 20 cm (8 in) long

Hylonomus, 20–25 cm (8–10 in) long

309 MILLION YEARS AGO

Essexella is the oldest definite fossilized **jellyfish**, although jellyfish almost certainly lived earlier. Their entirely soft, watery bodies mean that it is very difficult for jellyfish to fossilize.

While amphibians hatch from their eggs as larvae that look different from the adult form, reptiles hatch as smaller versions of the adult. Frogs, which are amphibians, hatch first as tadpoles and slowly change into their frog form. This would have been true of early amphibians, too.

307–299 MILLION YEARS AGO

The first plant-eating (herbivorous) four-legged animals were **reptiles**. Arthropods had been eating decaying and living plant matter for a long time, but amphibians ate fish and small arthropods.

309–307 MILLION YEARS AGO

Tullimonstrum, or **"Tully monster,"** was a strange, soft-bodied animal that lived in muddy estuaries where rivers joined a tropical sea. It had gills and a notochord (a stiff rod along the back). With fierce teeth in a long jaw and large eyes on stalks, it was almost certainly a predator.

Tullimonstrum,
35 cm (13.7 in)

306–255 MILLION YEARS AGO

An **amphibian** with a head strangely shaped like a boomerang, *Diplocaulus* lived in swamps and rivers. Its head might have helped the animal to swim at the surface, or perhaps it made *Diplocaulus* hard for larger animals to swallow.

Diplocaulus,
1 m (3.3 ft)

305 MILLION YEARS AGO

An extinction event saw the **collapse of the great rain forests**. Pockets of forest remained, but were dominated by seed ferns and tree ferns rather than scale trees like *Lepidodendron.*

300 MILLION YEARS AGO

Meganeura had a wingspan of over 75 cm (30 in)

306–280 MILLION YEARS AGO

Ophiacodon was an early **synapsid reptile**, one of the group from which mammals later evolved. It spent some time in the water, probably hunting animals that came to the edge to drink.

Ophiacodon grew to 3 m (9.8 ft) long and had more than 150 teeth.

305–299 MILLION YEARS AGO

Meganeura was a **giant flying insect**, something like a dragonfly but the size of a seagull. It is one of the largest flying insects there has ever been. *Meganeura* probably ate other insects and perhaps small amphibians.

Spinoequalis, 25 cm (10 in) long

300 MILLION YEARS AGO

Spinoequalis was the **first reptile to return to the water**, although it had to lay its eggs on land. Its tail was taller than it was wide, with flat sides, helping it to swim.

CHAPTER 3

THE RISE OF REPTILES

Amphibians and arthropods spread inland around rivers and the coast, but reptiles went farther. Freed from the need to stay near water to breed, they started to live in lots of different environments. Over millions of years, they grew to have different sizes, shapes, habits, and habitats (living spaces). Some of them eventually returned to the water, and others even took to the skies, evolving wings and beginning to fly. They changed in other ways, too, and from the reptiles the final two groups of land animals evolved: birds and mammals.

For around 60–70 million years, covering all of the Permian and the early Triassic periods, reptiles ruled the land. Only a few arthropods, such as dragonflies, could fly. The water was home to fish and amphibians. During this time, the land was grouped together in a supercontinent that we now call Pangea. Animals could walk all over the Earth since the land was joined together, and similar fossils are found in lands now widely separated.

A GOOD EGG

Animals that reproduce sexually (with the baby having two parents) can either lay eggs or give birth to live babies. Egg-laying was the first method and is used by fish, insects, amphibians, reptiles, birds, and a small group of mammals called "monotremes." Live birth has evolved many times over. Now, some fish, reptiles, and most mammals give birth to their babies. Even animals that give birth to live young have eggs, though. Their eggs develop into young inside the mother's body.

EGGS FOR WET LIVES

Fish and amphibians **lay their eggs in water**. This means the eggs will never dry out, so they don't need a thick or hard shell that water can't pass through. Instead, their eggs are jellylike, with a thin outer skin or "membrane." Amphibians have always needed to return to the water to lay their eggs, and they still do. A new type of egg was needed for animals to live in areas with little or no water, for laying their eggs on land. That new type of egg was produced by reptiles, and it freed them from the need to stay near water.

Fish eggs (above) and amphibian eggs like this frogspawn (left) are soft and squishy.

EGGS AND EGGSHELLS

The new type of eggs are called **"amniotic" eggs**, and the animals that produce them are "amniotes." Amphibian and fish eggs are soft and squishy, but the amniotic eggs laid by birds and reptiles have a hard or leathery outside called a **shell**. Inside, membranes (which are thin layers, like a layer of skin) enclose all the functional parts of the egg. The growing **embryo**, which will become the baby, and the yolk sac, which is the embryo's food source, are also surrounded by membranes. Today, some reptiles lay eggs with hard shells, while others lay eggs with a tough, leathery shell—and others give birth. All birds lay eggs with hard shells.

Birds lay amniotic eggs with hard, protective shells.

An amniotic egg has protective membranes inside. Air can pass through the shell.

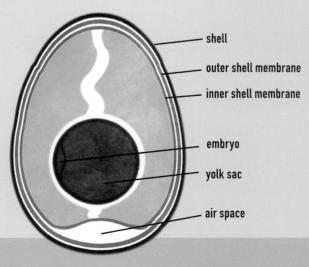

shell

outer shell membrane

inner shell membrane

embryo

yolk sac

air space

HUMANS AND OTHER AMNIOTES

Humans and other mammals are also amniotes, even though they don't lay eggs. Mammals have evolved to keep their fertilized eggs **inside the mother's body**. The eggs still have the same membranes, although the structure of the egg has changed a little. The egg is implanted in the uterus (womb) of the mother, and a placenta grows. This is a new organ, which nourishes the embryo and gets rid of its waste. Keeping the growing embryo inside the mother's body protects it from predators, changing conditions, and other dangers. A very small number of mammals lay eggs, and a few more called **"marsupials"** give birth to small, undeveloped babies that grow further in a pouch on the mother's body.

Stereopodon, like a modern duck-billed platypus, was a monotreme—an egg-laying mammal.

STRANGE BABIES

Amphibians not only lay soft, squishy eggs, they also have babies that have an immature **"larval" form** that looks unlike the adult animal. Frog babies are tadpoles, for example, with no legs and a long tail. The larvae live in the water all the time and can't breathe in air. As they grow, they go through a time of change called **"metamorphosis,"** when they get their adult body shape. As a tadpole grows, it gets first back legs, then front legs, and finally its tail shrinks away. Its body changes in less obvious ways, too, as the gills it used to breathe in water give way to lungs for breathing in air.

When a baby reptile or bird hatches, it looks much like the adult with just small differences. A bird might hatch helpless and with no feathers. Babies often have different proportions from adults, such as a larger head and larger eyes. But all its limbs are in place, and nothing will be added or removed (except perhaps feathers or fur). It can breathe air immediately.

A frog has babies with bodies entirely different from the adult form. The tadpole lives only in water and can't breathe air.

A baby crocodile hatches already looking like a miniature version of an adult crocodile.

299–276 MILLION YEARS AGO

As the huge landmass of Pangea formed, the land farthest from the sea became very dry. Rain fell near the coast but was not carried far inland. The great rain forests of the Carboniferous died, giving way to a different type of landscape and climate—one that favored the reptiles, with their eggs that could tolerate dry conditions.

299–253 MILLION YEARS AGO

Archegosaurus was **closer to a fish than an amphibian** in many ways—despite having legs! It spent all its time in water and had gills to breathe like a fish. Around 1.5 m (5 ft) long, it looked something like a crocodile.

299–278 MILLION YEARS AGO

Eryops was a large, early amphibian. It had a skeleton made entirely of bone, which meant it **fossilized easily** and many examples have been found. Many other early amphibians had skeletons partly made of cartilage. *Eryops* ate fish, and small reptiles and amphibians.

Eryops,
2 m (6.6 ft) long

299 MILLION YEARS AGO

299–252 MILLION YEARS AGO

As the inland parts of Pangea became drier and cooler, conifers and **seed ferns** like *Glossopteris* took over from tropical trees. Huge forests of glossopterids (plants related to *Glossopteris*) spread across much of the land in the south.

Glossopteris,
4–8 m (13–26 ft) tall

Glossopteris fossils are found in lands now widely separated by oceans. They are a key piece of evidence that continents have moved around over time. Bands of *Glossopteris* fossils that span South America, South Africa, Australia, India, and Antarctica show that these lands were once joined, then split after the trees had died, since their seeds would not cross the oceans.

299–280 MILLION YEARS AGO

Freshwater **lungfish** and sharks swam in the inland rivers. Lungfish became more diverse (varied) and larger, but they gradually reduced in numbers.

Ceratodus, 50 cm (20 in)

295 MILLION YEARS AGO

Beetles and flies became common, probably feeding on rotting wood and boring into living wood.

295–272 MILLION YEARS AGO

Early **"stem mammals"** like *Dimetrodon* were animals that had developed some features that were later common in mammals, but they were not yet mammals. *Dimetrodon* was a savage carnivore with a large sail supported on its back by bony spines. The sail might have been to impress a possible mate or perhaps used to keep the animal's temperature stable. It could stand with its sail exposed to sunlight to warm up, or turned toward a breeze to cool down.

Diadectes,
1.5–3 m (5–10 ft) long

290–272 MILLION YEARS AGO

For the first time, some tetrapods began to **eat plants** and **grow larger**. Among the first was the *Diadectes*, which had some features of reptiles and some of amphibians. It had nipping teeth at the front of its mouth and chewing teeth farther back, adapted to eating tough plant matter. The smaller *Orobates* possibly made **burrows** to hide from the dry heat of the day. Animals like these spread widely, taking advantage of their amniotic eggs to move into places amphibians could not survive.

Dimetrodon,
3.5 m (11.5 ft)

Orobates, 1 m (3.3 ft)

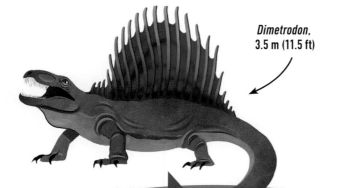

276 MILLION YEARS AGO

Varanops, 1.2 m (4 ft)

290–250 MILLION YEARS AGO

Life continued in the sea, with strange **sharks** like *Helicoprion* emerging. This had a bizarre curled roll of teeth in its lower jaw called a "tooth whorl."

Helicoprion is known only from the tooth whorl and head, so its size is not certain, but was probably up to 7.5 m (25 ft).

280–272.5 MILLION YEARS AGO

Varanops was an **active carnivore** that probably ate other reptiles and possibly amphibians. It had long legs suited to chasing prey over open ground and 220 sharp, curved teeth. *Varanops* was a synapsid, one of the group of reptiles from which mammals eventually evolved.

280–270 MILLION YEARS AGO

The reptile-like *Seymouria* was an **amphibian adapted well for life on land**, but it probably returned to the water to spawn (produce eggs). It was a carnivore, eating invertebrates and smaller amphibians.

Seymouria,
60 cm (2 ft)

275–252 MILLION YEARS AGO

The rise of stem mammals continued, bringing a world (on land) in which a small number of predators fed on a much larger number of herbivores. Carnivores became better adapted to hunting, with long limbs for fast running, teeth of different shapes for piercing, gripping, ripping, and chewing, eyes facing forward for good stereoscopic vision, and improved hearing.

Moschops, 2.5 m (8 ft) long, had a skull up to 10 cm (4 in) thick.

273 MILLION YEARS AGO

A **mass extinction event** changed the balance of animals living on land, killing around two-thirds of them.

268–252 MILLION YEARS AGO

Suminia was the first known tetrapod (four-footed animal) to **live in trees**. Its teeth show that it ate leaves, and its limbs were adapted to grasping and clinging to branches, with possibly a "toe thumb" as well as a thumb on the hands. The tail would have helped it to balance and was possibly prehensile—capable of being used to grip.

265–260 MILLION YEARS AGO

Moschops was a **plant-eating dinocephalian**, sturdily built and strong. It had thick bone at the top of its skull, possibly an adaptation for head-butting or other social activity. Some modern animals bash their heads against each other in battles to decide which will lead a herd or win a mate.

275 MILLION YEARS AGO

270 MILLION YEARS AGO

Some synapsids evolved into **therapsids**, which were the ancestors of all modern mammals. Some even grew hair or fur. The synapsids (like *Dimetrodon*) began to die out.

270–260 MILLION YEARS AGO

Reefs created by algae grew on the edges of inland seas that were connected by channels to the ocean. These dried out around 252 million years ago as sea levels fell, leaving vast salt flats and killing the marine life of the reefs.

268–265 MILLION YEARS AGO

A group of reptiles called **dinocephalians** evolved with large bodies and heads. There were both plant-eaters and meat-eaters, and they were among the largest land animals of their time. *Titanophoneus* was a typical carnivorous dinocephalian, with frightening-looking teeth. Its legs splayed out to the side, giving it a slow, sprawling gait. It probably ambushed and bit its prey, then waited for it to die instead of chasing after it.

Titanophoneus, 3–5 m (10–16.5 ft)

260–247 MILLION YEARS AGO

Coelocanthus was a large, **lobe-finned fish that lived in the open seas** around areas that are now Germany and England. Coelocanths survived the next three mass extinctions.

260–252 MILLION YEARS AGO

Scutosaurus was an armored herbivore of a type called a **pareiasaur**. About the size of a cow, it was the first animal known to have legs that came out directly under the body, like modern mammals. A large belly held a long gut for breaking down tough plants. Pareiasaurs were the largest Permian land animals. Many had bony nobbles or plates called "osteoderms" for protection against predators.

Scutosaurus, 2.5 m (8 ft) long, may have roamed in groups. It had good hearing and could possibly bellow to communicate with its fellows.

Stem mammals had legs coming from directly under the trunk, rather than splayed out to the side as they are in amphibians. Legs like this are better for running quickly and helped both predators and escaping prey. The most mammal-like were a group called cynodonts, which means "dog-toothed." Some probably hunted in packs, might have had whiskers and some type of hair, and were endothermic (warm-blooded and able to control their own body temperatures). The cynodonts were ancestors to modern mammals.

Animals with a sprawling gait have legs that stick out to the side of their bodies (below). Dinosaurs and mammals have an upright gait, with legs vertically beneath their bodies (right).

252 MILLION YEARS AGO

260–254 MILLION YEARS AGO

Not all reptiles were large. *Diictodon* and *Robertia* were smaller. Both were dicynodonts, with **large canine teeth** or tusks. Their tusks were probably used for digging up roots to eat. Besides the tusks, they had a hard beak for snipping through plants, but no other teeth.

Diictodon, 1 m (3.3 ft) long, dug burrows.

Robertia, 40 cm (16 in) long

260–251 MILLION YEARS AGO

Coelurosauravus was among the first animals besides insects to take to the air. A **gliding lizard**, it could sail between trees on flaps of skin supported by bony rods. Its wings extended from its front limbs to its hips.

Coelurosauravus, 40 cm (16 in) long

252 MILLION YEARS AGO

The most devastating mass extinction event of all time **ended the Permian period.**

GOODBYE TO ALL THESE

The Permian period ended with a catastrophic mass extinction event, the worst the world has ever seen. It killed around 95 per cent of all species on Earth, leaving the land and sea largely deserted and uninhabitable.

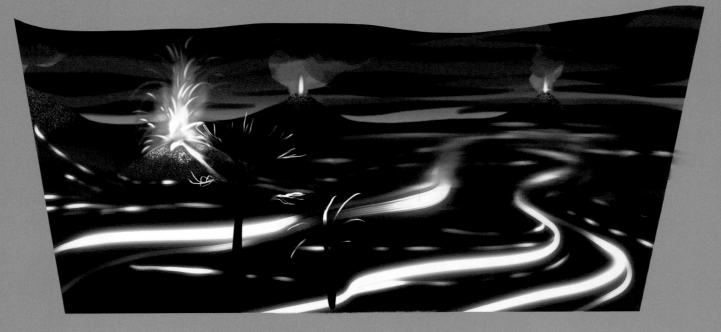

BAD TIMES

Most experts think that the mass extinction was caused by **huge volcanic eruptions** in Siberia (now part of northern Russia). These were not mountainous volcanoes, but vast plains of lava flooding molten rock over the ground for 100,000 years or more. The eruptions released enough lava to cover the entire Earth to a depth of 6 m (20 ft), but in fact covered Siberia with a layer 4 km (2.5 miles) deep.

Each bout of eruptions filled the sky with ash, gases, and dust, darkening and cooling Earth and causing acid rain. Plants and trees all died. With no roots to hold it in place, soil washed away into the sea, carrying dead plants and animals with it. Sea levels dropped in the cold, drying up shallow seas and killing the organisms that lived in them. Dead matter carried into the sea and gases in the atmosphere stripped seawater of oxygen, killing plankton and fish. But that was just the first stage.

FROM COLD TO HOT

Cold was followed by heat. Methane produced by microbes breaking down rotting plant and animal matter, and gases from the volcanic eruptions, led to a **greenhouse effect** and warming. With no leaves to take the carbon dioxide out of the air, conditions got worse. Earth grew as much as 15° C (28° F) hotter.

CONSEQUENCES

Extinction events cause a cascade of deaths. If plants and trees are destroyed, the animals that eat them die, then the animals that eat the plant-eaters die. When soil is washed away, the worms and insects are lost, too. When the sea is flooded with debris and stripped of oxygen, the plants and fish die. The rotting dead things make sea conditions even worse. The mass extinction at the end of the Permian has been called the **"Great Dying"** because so many species disappeared.

Trilobites, such as *Ditomopyge*, survived for 270 million years, but were wiped out in the "Great Dying."

SURVIVORS

Yet, there were survivors. A mass extinction is good for one type of organism: **decomposers**. The microbes, fungi, and small animals such as worms and arthropods that break down dead and rotting material had a feast. The fossil record shows a rise in the number of **fungi**.

A few **larger organisms** survived, too. On land, *Lystrosaurus* was a survivor. It could adapt to different climates and conditions, and with less competition from other animals, it spread from Russia to Antarctica, dominating the land. Slowly, the surviving species spread out, adapted to the conditions they found in new places, and evolved into new species. Even so, it took perhaps 10 million years for Earth to recover the diversity it had before the Great Dying.

Lystrosaurus

251–245 MILLION YEARS AGO

The period after the Great Dying was a crucial time in the evolution of vertebrates (animals with backbones). The next period, the Triassic, brought reptiles called archosaurs, from which dinosaurs, pterosaurs, crocodiles, and later birds evolved. It also saw the first mammals. As Earth came out of the disaster, it was very hot and mostly dry. Sea levels were high, and there was no ice at the poles. All the land was still joined, but it began to separate as Pangea broke apart.

251–250 MILLION YEARS AGO

After the Great Dying, almost all animals were small. One of the **largest carnivores** was *Proterosuchus*. It hunted by both land and water—being adaptable helped it survive.

Proterosuchus.
1-2 m (3.3–6.6 ft)

Brachiopod   Bivalve

251 MILLION YEARS AGO

Before the extinction, **brachiopods** were the main filter-feeders on the seabed. Afterward, they were largely replaced by **bivalves** with their two-part hinged shells.

251 MILLION YEARS AGO

Trematosaurus.
2–3 m (6.6–10 ft)

251–247 MILLION YEARS AGO

Thrinaxodon was a carnivore about the size of a fox. A **stem mammal**, it had some mammal-like features including legs that came out directly under its body and possibly a covering of hair. It probably survived the terrible conditions after the extinction event by being able to burrow and hide away when necessary.

Thrinaxodon.
45 cm (18 in)

251–247 MILLION YEARS AGO

Trematosaurus was a **large amphibian** that looked something like a crocodile. It lived in the sea and brackish (slightly salty) water. With eyes and nostrils on top of its head, it could lie mostly submerged while still breathing and seeing above the water. It ate fish and other animals.

250 MILLION YEARS AGO

Crinoids were almost wiped out in the Great Dying, but they made a comeback. New types of crinoid emerged, some with up to 300 arms.

Crinoids attached to the seafloor with a "standfast."

251 MILLION YEARS AGO

As plants recovered, much of the land was covered with conifers. Some of these trees grew to 30 m (98 ft) tall. Later in the Triassic, as the climate and land became drier, many of the forests were replaced with huge plains covered with ferns.

250 MILLION YEARS AGO

Small amphibians of the same type as **frogs and salamanders** began to appear. Most amphibians were much larger.

249–237 MILLION YEARS AGO

Cymbospondylus was an early **ichthyosaur**—a fish-shaped reptile that lived in the sea and never went onto land. Ichthyosaurs quickly evolved to very large sizes after the Great Dying. *Cymbospondylus* grew to 10 m (33 ft), but the later *Shastasaurus* was even bigger at 21 m (69 ft).

Despite its size, *Cymbospondylus* ate only small to medium-sized fish, ammonites, and belemnites (animals like a squid).

245 MILLION YEARS AGO

Mesosuchus, 30 cm (1 ft)

246 MILLION YEARS AGO

Mesosuchus was a **rhynchosaur**, one of the groups that emerged in the Triassic and disappeared again, leaving no living types. Most rhynchosaurs ate plants. They had a beak like a parrot's and several rows of small teeth for crushing and grinding plants. Many were sturdy, piglike animals, and all had a broad head.

245 MILLION YEARS AGO

The group of reptiles called **archosaurs** divided into two types. One type, which went on to include birds and dinosaurs, had a hinged ankle joint (like your knee joint). The other type, which includes crocodiles, had a ball-and-socket joint in the ankle (like your shoulder joint).

Placodus, 2 m (6.6 ft)

Euparkeria, 70 cm (2.3 ft), was a fast runner with a good sense of smell.

245–230 MILLION YEARS AGO

A relative of archosaurs, *Euparkeria* had some **features of later dinosaurs**. It had bony plates called osteoderms along its back and tail, a mouth full of sharp, spiny teeth, and long back legs that it could stand up on occasionally. It lived near the South Pole and had good nighttime vision to cope with long, dark winters.

245–235 MILLION YEARS AGO

Placodus was a **marine (seagoing) reptile that could still move on land** when it needed to, but would have been slow and cumbersome. It lived near the coast, plucking shellfish from the seabed with its forward-facing front teeth, and crunching through the shells with rows of flat, crushing teeth across the back of its mouth.

BACK TO THE WATER

Life began in the water, then some organisms ventured onto land—but some returned to the water. All this time, there were still many organisms that had never left the sea, and others that moved from the sea into brackish waters near the coast and freshwater inland.

NICE AND WET

Tetrapods (animals with four legs) that moved onto land became **amphibians**, but they never fully left the water. Even now, amphibians need to lay their eggs in water, and their young live in water. Many continued to catch their food in the water. Others evolved into **reptiles** and cut all ties with water—for a while. From the Triassic, some animals that were fully adapted to life on land began to return to the water.

FIRST IN THE WATER

The first reptiles to return to the water were nothosaurs and ichthyosaurs. Both these, like all other water-going reptiles, still needed to breathe air, so they had to come frequently to the surface. No marine reptiles could live in the deepest parts of the ocean.

Nothosaurs had webbed feet for swimming but could haul themselves over rocks, as seals can now. They probably spent a lot of time on land, but hunted in the sea. Their spiny, outward-pointing teeth were adapted to catch and hold slippery fish, but they also ate other marine reptiles smaller than themselves. It isn't known whether they came on land to lay eggs, or whether they gave birth in the water. All nothosaurs died out in an extinction event at the end of the Triassic.

Nothosaurus, 4 m (13 ft), lived 240–210 million years ago.

Mixosaurus, an ichthyosaur, was 1 m (3.3 ft) long.

Ichthyosaurs were fish-shaped marine reptiles. They evolved from land-going reptiles that went back into the sea. Their limbs became more like paddles, often fin-shaped. Their heads became a more streamlined shape for cutting through the water, and the shape of the body was smooth and curved. They could use their tail as a rudder or to help them move.

BABIES IN THE WATER

At least some ichthyosaurs **gave birth to live babies**, so they never had to make their way onto land. These animals were so well adapted to life in the water that it would have been almost impossible for them to move on land. When the baby was born, the mother would have helped it to the surface to take its first breath, just as modern marine mammals like whales and dolphins do now.

A fossil of the ichthyosaur *Stenopterygius* giving birth shows that the babies emerged tail first. The mother would have helped the newborn to the surface to breathe.

SIMILAR SHAPES

The shapes that ichthyosaurs and nothosaurs developed are similar to the shapes of fish and seals, but they are not related to these animals. Evolution led them to have the same shape because those shapes are well suited to life in the water. This is called **"convergent evolution"**: Unrelated organisms evolve similar features from different starting points, because those features are suited to the conditions the organism lives in.

***Hupehsuchus*, 1 m (3.3 ft), lived 251–247 million years ago and was not related to ichthyosaurs, but evolved a similar shape.**

A dolphin has separately evolved a shape similar to that of ichthyosaurs and fish.

244–220 MILLION YEARS AGO

Once life got going again after the Great Dying, it began to diversify in new directions. The middle Triassic saw the appearance of the first mammals and the first dinosaurs. Both began small, but dinosaurs would soon grow much larger.

Henodus,
1 m (3.3 ft)

242 MILLION YEARS AGO

The odd reptile *Tanystropheus* had a **neck up to 3 m (10 ft) long**, taking up more than half its entire length. It lived in the sea, probably hunting fish in murky water where its large body could stay hidden.

Tanystropheus,
5 m (16 ft)

237–227 MILLION YEARS AGO

Henodus looked like a giant, flattened turtle, with a shell wider than it was long. Unlike a turtle's shell, it was made of **overlapping, fused bony plates**. *Henodus* had just two teeth. It probably fed by filtering plant matter from the water and perhaps scraping algae from rocks or the seabed.

244 MILLION YEARS AGO

241–236 MILLION YEARS AGO

Prestosuchus was a type of reptile called a **rauisuchian**. These large, predatory animals looked like heavy crocodiles, with a big head crammed with ferocious teeth. Some rauisuchians grew to 10 m (33 ft) long. They were the apex (top) predators of the Triassic. *Prestosuchus* walked on four legs, but some other rauisuchians more often walked on their two hind legs.

Prestosuchus, 6.5 m (21 ft)

240 MILLION YEARS AGO

The Permian corals were all gone, but new **coral-building animals** related to modern coral polyps appeared—animals like tiny sea anemones that build a hard shell around themselves. At first, they didn't build reefs, but lived alone in shallow seas.

230 MILLION YEARS AGO

The **first mammals** appeared, small at first. The shrewlike *Eozostrodon*, around 10 cm (4 in) long, was one of the earliest. The mother produced milk for her babies like modern mammals, but the babies hatched from eggs. Monotremes, such as the echidna, are the only mammals that still lay eggs.

231–229 MILLION YEARS AGO

One of the **first dinosaurs**, *Herrerasaurus* lived on land that is now South America. Light and agile, it was about 1 m (3.3 ft) tall to the hip. It was probably a very early theropod—the same type of dinosaur as *Tyrannosaurus rex*. Theropods walked on two legs and ate meat.

Herrerasaurus,
3–6 m (10–19.6 ft)

225 MILLION YEARS AGO

Saturnalia was a knee-high **sauropodomorph** dinosaur, meaning that it had a sauropod-shaped body. Sauropods later grew to enormous sizes in animals such as *Diplodocus* and *Argentinosaurus*.

Saturnalia, 2 m (6.6 ft)

220 MILLION YEARS AGO

The **rhynchosaurs**—beaked herbivorous reptiles—became extinct after flourishing for 25 million years.

Hyperodapedon, 1.3 m (4.2 ft) long, lived 231–227 million years ago and died out when the seed ferns it ate became extinct.

220 MILLION YEARS AGO

Slender and low compared to *Postosuchus*, the **crocodile-like** *Parasuchus* had a sprawling gait and ate fish.

Parasuchus, 2.5 m (8 ft)

220 MILLION YEARS AGO

Placerias, 3.5 m (11.4 ft), was a dicynodont reptile with some mammal-like features.

221–203 MILLION YEARS AGO

The rauisuchian *Postosuchus* lived alongside and probably ate the early theropod dinosaurs. With powerful biting muscles and dagger-like teeth up to 7 cm (2.8 in) long in a strong head, it was an **apex predator**. It could possibly choose whether to go on two or four legs. Bony scales called osteoderms protected its back and neck.

Postosuchus, 4.6 m (15 ft)

220–216 MILLION YEARS AGO

Placerias was one of the **largest Triassic herbivores**; it was the size and weight of a modern hippopotamus. It roamed in large herds over land that is now north America.

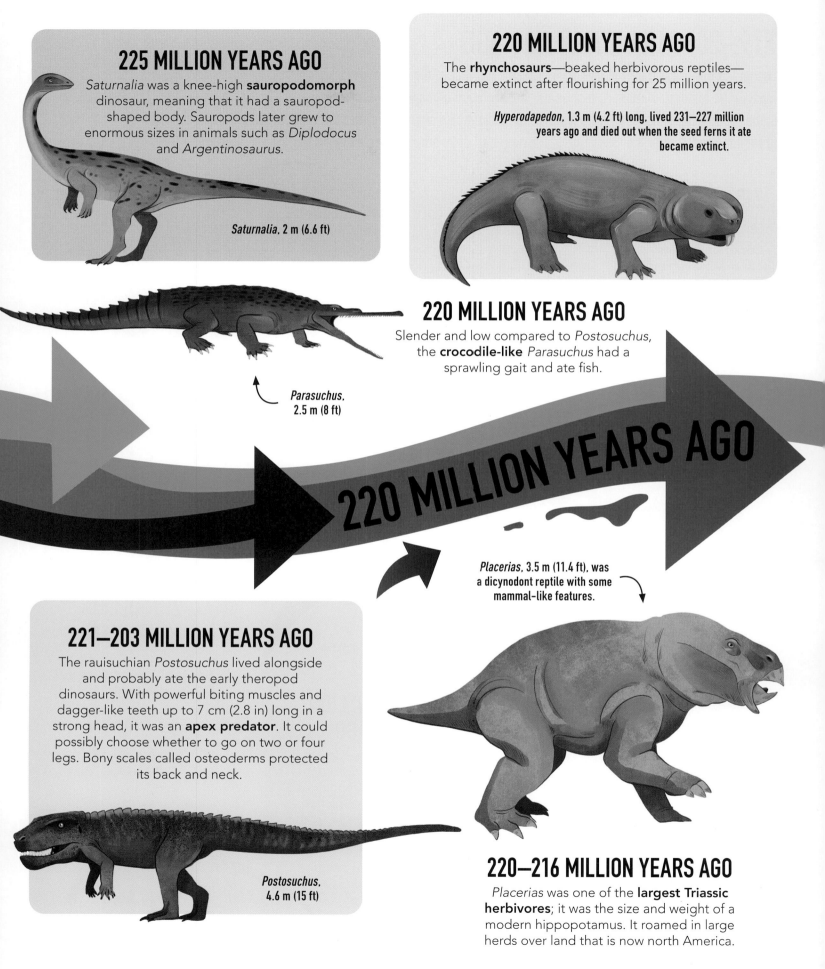

219–201 MILLION YEARS AGO

The end of the Triassic period saw an increasing number of dinosaurs and also the first mammals that had most of the features of modern mammals. The evolution of mammals was a slow process that began with some reptile-like animals gaining features later mammals shared. It ended with the mammals rising to great importance after the extinction of the non-bird dinosaurs 65.5 million years ago.

215–202 MILLION YEARS AGO

Corals built reefs rather than living independently. The coral polyps began a symbiotic (mutually helpful) relationship with algae that lived inside them. The algae produced food for the coral polyp by photosynthesizing.

210 MILLION YEARS AGO

One of the **last placodonts**, *Psephoderma* had a shell made of fused bony scutes. The shell was divided into two parts, one over the upper body and one over the hips. It used its pointy, beaklike nose to dig crustaceans out of the mud of the seabed or between rocks, and crushed them with teeth in the back of its mouth.

Psephoderma, 1.8 m (5 ft)

219 MILLION YEARS AGO

214–204 MILLION YEARS AGO

Plateosaurus was an **early sauropodomorph**. It ate plants, but sauropodomorphs at some point had evolved from meat-eating ancestors. *Plateosaurus* probably walked on its two hind legs most of the time, but later sauropods would grow so large that they had to walk on four legs. It had large claws on the front legs, possibly used to defend itself, as well as to pull plants toward its mouth.

Eudimorphodon, wingspan 1 m (3.3 ft)

210–205 MILLION YEARS AGO

The first **pterosaurs** appeared in the skies over Europe's coasts. These flying reptiles had wings of skin stretching from an elongated fourth finger to the rear legs, and a long tail. The mouth, packed with sharp teeth and fangs, was adapted to catching and eating fish and crustaceans.

Plateosaurus, 5–10 m (16–32 ft) long

210 MILLION YEARS AGO

Liliensternus was one of **largest Triassic theropods**. Much more lightly built than later giants like *Tyrannosaurus rex*, *Liliensternus* could run fast. It lived in the same area as *Plateosaurus* and probably hunted it.

Liliensternus, 5 m (16 ft)

205 MILLION YEARS AGO

The archosaur *Effigia* looked much like a theropod dinosaur, but features of its skeleton, such as the shape of its ankle, show it is related instead to the **ancestors of crocodiles**. Convergent evolution led it to develop the long, slender body, long legs, and clawed hands common in theropods.

Effigia, 2–3 m (6.6–10 ft) long, ran on two legs and had a toothless beak.

205 MILLION YEARS AGO

The **largest known ichthyosaur** was probably similar to *Shonisaurus*, which lived 237–227 million years ago. Only a fragment of the larger ichthyosaur has been found, but it seems to be from an animal 26 m (85 ft) long—nearly as large as a blue whale.

Shonisaurus, 15 m (49 ft)

205 MILLION YEARS AGO

The **first crocodilian reptiles** evolved from archosaurs like *Postosuchus*. These were the ancestors of modern crocodiles.

201 MILLION YEARS AGO

Thecodontosaurus, 2 m (6.6 ft) long, had an unusually short neck for a sauropodomorph.

205 MILLION YEARS AGO

One of the **earliest true mammals**, *Morganucodon* was small and shrewlike. It ate insects and was probably nocturnal (active at night), spending the daytime in a burrow. Like modern monotremes, *Morganucodon* laid eggs, but probably also produced milk for its young.

Morganucodon, 9 cm (4 in)

204–201 MILLION YEARS AGO

Thecodontosaurus was a skinny, **plant-eating sauropodomorph**. Many *Thecodontosaurus* fossils are found in cracks in limestone rocks in southern England, where they perhaps fell while searching for food or were killed by rockfalls.

201 MILLION YEARS AGO

The **end-Triassic extinction event** killed off the crocodile-like phytosaurs, large amphibians, and synapsids. In the sea, coral reefs were wiped out. The cause was probably volcanic eruptions pouring carbon dioxide into the air and so warming the planet. Land plants, dinosaurs, mammals, and pterosaurs survived well.

THE RISE OF DINOSAURS

Although the dinosaurs first appeared during the Triassic, they were one player among many. Large, fierce archosaurs such as *Postosuchus* were the apex predators. It took another mass extinction event to clear the way for the dinosaurs to grow larger and rise to dominate the world.

CLEARING A PATH

By killing many of the archosaurs, the **mass extinction at the end of the Triassic** left spaces on land for surviving organisms to expand and diversify. The most successful of the lucky survivors were the dinosaurs and pterosaurs. The mammals also survived, but they remained small for a long time yet.

Like other early dinosaurs, *Scutellosaurus* was small and nimble, and ran on two feet.

BECOMING A DINOSAUR

The change from archosaurs to dinosaurs was marked especially by **changes in the legs and hips** (see page 53). The early dinosaurs ran on two legs, and they needed changes to their skeleton to make that possible. Their legs came down directly under their bodies (like a modern mammal such as a cow or dog), whereas those of archosaurs and modern reptiles such as crocodiles stick out to the sides.

The **first dinosaurs** probably appeared around 240 million years ago. The earliest dinosaur might be *Nyasaurus*, found in Africa—or this might be a late dinosaur ancestor, just before the dinosaurs emerged. So little remains of *Nyasaurus* it's impossible to be certain. The earliest dinosaurs were no more than 2 m (6.6 ft) long, ran on two legs, and ate meat or insects. They might have sometimes nibbled plants, but they were not mostly plant-eaters.

Nyasaurus lived 240 million years ago—but was it a dinosaur or just almost a dinosaur?

DIFFERENT HIPS

As dinosaurs evolved, they developed two different styles of hips, forming two groups often called **"lizard-hipped dinosaurs"** and **"bird-hipped dinosaurs."** Oddly, birds evolved from lizard-hipped dinosaurs.

Theropods like *Tyrannosaurus rex* were lizard-hipped dinosaurs (top), while ornithischians like *Corythosaurus* were bird-hipped dinosaurs.

WALKING STYLE

During the Triassic and then the Jurassic and Cretaceous, dinosaurs evolved to have three characteristic types with related body shapes. **Theropods** walked on two legs and ate meat. **Sauropods** walked on four legs and ate plants. **Ornithischians** were a mixed bag. Some walked on two legs and some on four. They ranged from the low, squat animals that always went on four legs (like *Triceratops*, below) to lighter, more nimble animals that could go on two legs like *Gasparinisaura*—but they all ate plants.

Characteristic shapes of theropods (top), sauropods (middle), and ornithischians (bottom).

GROWING UP

Through the Triassic, dinosaurs remained **small**. Many were fast and agile, like *Coelophysis*, with jaws packed full of needle-sharp teeth. These were the ancestors of the huge theropod dinosaurs like *Allosaurus* and *Tyrannosaurus rex*. Another group called sauropodomorphs evolved from animals only a few meters long to become **giants** like *Diplodocus*, which could be more than 24 m (79 ft) long. But these giants wouldn't arrive until the Jurassic, when the end-Triassic extinction had cleared space for the dinosaurs to take over.

***Coelophysis* probably ate insects and small reptiles.**

CHAPTER 4

AGE OF DINOSAURS

From the beginning of the Jurassic 201 million years ago until the end of the Cretaceous 65.5 million years ago, the dinosaurs were unchallenged rulers of Earth. They lived everywhere, and their fossils are found on all continents, even Antarctica. They ranged from animals smaller than a chicken to the largest land animals there have ever been. Some had feathers, and others had scaly skin. Some had bony plates, spikes, spines, dagger-like claws, or soaring sails. Some had hundreds of teeth, and others had no teeth at all. Some ate plants, others ate insects, small reptiles, fish, or other dinosaurs. They were all reptiles and laid eggs. At the same time, the skies were home to flying reptiles, the pterosaurs. Plesiosaurs and pliosaurs swam with the ichthyosaurs in the seas. They were all marine reptiles.

201–170 MILLION YEARS AGO

The supercontinent Pangea began to split into north and south landmasses, the Tethys Ocean opening between them. Land animals and plants could still move east and west in each land block, but they could no longer move between north and south. They began to evolve separately, with once-identical organisms becoming new species suited to different living conditions.

201–191 MILLION YEARS AGO

Many **pterosaurs** had no teeth, but *Dimorphodon* was unusual in having two different styles of teeth. It had larger teeth in the top of the mouth and more, smaller teeth in the bottom jaw. It might have caught insects or small animals, or perhaps snapped fish from the sea.

Dimorphodon, 1.5 m (5 ft) wingspan

200–183 MILLION YEARS AGO

The **sauropodomorph** *Massospondylus* walked on its hind legs as an adult, but its babies walked on all fours. The front limbs had five fingers, with large, curved thumb claws. It seems that *Massospondylus* grew larger when there was more food available and remained a smaller size if food was scarce.

Massospondylus, 4–6 m (13–20 ft)

201 MILLION YEARS AGO

Belemnite, from 50 cm (20 in) to 3 m (10 ft)

Williamsonia grew 2 m (6.5 ft) tall, with a flower 10 cm (4 in) long

200 MILLION YEARS AGO

Belemnites had a squid-like body, but unlike modern squids, they had an interior skeleton in the form of a bullet-shaped "rostrum" at the end opposite the tentacles. Fossilized rostra are commonly found. Belemnites survived for 135 million years, dying out with the dinosaurs.

200 MILLION YEARS AGO

Williamsonia had a thick, scaly trunk below a crown of large leaf fronds. These surrounded a large flowerlike structure that held **seeds on stalks**. It became common in the Jurassic, after first appearing in the late Triassic.

200–170 MILLION YEARS AGO

The plant *Schmeissneria* might have been the earliest **flowering plant** (or "angiosperm"). The flowers looked like small tufts of hair.

199–196 MILLION YEARS AGO

One of the earliest **ornithischian dinosaurs** was *Heterodontosaurus*. Possibly covered with hair-like feathers, it had five digits on each hand, two of which were opposable—so could be used like thumbs. *Heterodontosaurus* was unusual in having three different types of teeth: tusks, slicing teeth at the front of the mouth, and grinding teeth at the back. We don't know what it ate, though.

Heterodontosaurus,
1.2–1.8 m (4–6 ft) long

184 MILLION YEARS AGO

One of the earliest **armored dinosaurs**, *Scutellosaurus*, was a small ornithischian with bony plates along its back. This gave it some protection against predators. Later, armored dinosaurs became large and varied, ranging from *Stegosaurus* to the tank-like *Ankylosaurus*.

Scutellosaurus,
1.2 m (4 ft) long

170 MILLION YEARS AGO

193 MILLION YEARS AGO

Just 15 cm (6 in) long, *Sinocodon* was a very early mammal-like animal on the **border between stem mammal and mammal**. It probably looked like a rodent, but laid eggs and did not produce milk for its babies. It had the jaw bone arrangement of mammals.

193 MILLION YEARS AGO

New types of marine reptiles, **plesiosaurs and pliosaurs**, first appeared in the sea at the end of the Triassic. *Plesiosaurus* was an early plesiosaur and the first discovered. It moved through the water using four paddle-like flippers, evolved from land-going feet. It probably spent all its time in the water and gave birth to live young. With a long neck and a mouthful of needle-sharp teeth, it fed mostly on clams and snails that it plucked from the seabed and rocks, but it could also eat belemnites and fish.

190 MILLION YEARS AGO

Posalirus was the earliest **ancestor of frogs** that looked and jumped like a modern frog.

Forms of gingko survive today, and they were eaten by dinosaurs 100 million years ago.

170 MILLION YEARS AGO—NOW

Gingko trees became widespread in the middle of the Jurassic, although the very first types appeared much earlier, around 290 million years ago. They had soft leaves and no flowers, and grew near streams.

Plesiosaurus,
3.5 m (11.5 ft)

TAKE TO THE SKIES

The first flying animals were insects, which grew large and plentiful in the Carboniferous swamps and forests. They had the skies to themselves until the Jurassic, but by the end of the Jurassic 145 million years ago, they had been joined by gliding mammals, pterosaurs, and the first birds. All evolved flight independently but pterosaurs were the first.

REPTILES IN THE SKY

Pterosaurs first appeared around 210 million years ago and were hugely successful in the time of the dinosaurs, but all went extinct 65.5 million years ago. They ranged in size from no bigger than a small bird to taller than a giraffe. They were most diverse (varied) around 125 million years ago, in the Cretaceous. Although they all had large heads, often larger than the body, the skull had large holes, and the bones were thin and hollow, keeping the animal's weight down for flying. Like birds, they laid eggs, but with soft, leathery shells rather than the hard shells of bird eggs.

The Jurassic pterosaur *Pterodactylus* had a stumpy tail and small head crest.

TEETH AND TAILS

The earliest pterosaurs, like *Eudimorphodon*, had **teeth** adapted to eating small animals, including arthropods. Later, many lived by the coast and fed on fish. The teeth of fish-eaters were often sharp and snaggly, suited to grabbing and holding onto a slithery meal that would struggle to get away. Other pterosaurs had no teeth at all. The huge *Quetzalcoatlus* was toothless and probably hunted on land, something like a modern stork, snatching up small vertebrates in a gulp. The most famous, *Pterodactylus*, ate invertebrates and had a strong bite to crunch through their hard outsides.

While the early pterosaurs had long **tails**, often with a kite-shaped "vane" at the end, later pterosaurs lost their tails and had only a short stump.

One of the earliest pterosaurs, *Eudimorphodon* (210–203 million years ago), had a wingspan of 1 m (3.3 ft) and weighed around 10 kg (22 lb).

Rhamphorhychus (151–148.5 million years ago) had a mouthful of snaggly, needle-sharp teeth for snatching and trapping fish, and a kite-shaped end to its long tail.

Liaodactylus (160 million years ago) filtered water through a comb-like collection of tiny teeth packed close together. It had only a short tail.

WINGS AND WACKY WALKING

Unlike birds, which walk on just their hind legs keeping their wings off the ground, pterosaurs were quadrupedal which means they **walked on all fours**. The **wings** folded back at the last joint, the last part of the wing being a greatly extended fourth finger. The wings were flaps of skin that stretched between the finger bones and the rear legs. Pterosaurs never perched in trees, having feet unsuitable for gripping branches. They probably launched themselves into the air with a strong jump using all four feet.

The body was covered in fuzzy hair called **pycnofibers**. These were neither deeply rooted in the skin like the hair of mammals, nor complex in structure like feathers. They probably kept the animal warm.

Quetzalcoatlus (68–65.5 million years ago) was the largest pterosaur, with a wingspan of 11 m (33 ft) and a height of 3 m (9.8 ft) to the shoulder when standing. It probably fed on small animals, which it swallowed whole since it had no teeth.

Tupandactylus (112 million years ago) had a huge head crest.

PRETTY HEADS

Many pterosaurs had **ornate head crests**. These might have been used for species recognition, so that pterosaurs of the same type could easily identify each other, and maybe to attract and impress a mate. Some, like *Tupandactylus*, had crests so large they look as if they might have been a nuisance. Today, male peacocks have large tails which serve no function other than to attract a mate, and these must make movement more difficult for the bird. It's possible that the crest helped to stabilize the animal in the air or water.

We don't know whether there was always a membrane between bones of crests like that of *Nyctosaurus* (86–72 million years ago).

Crest with membrane

Crest with just bones

155–145 MILLION YEARS AGO

The late Jurassic was the time of some of the most famous dinosaurs. It was also a warm time, when there was less temperature variation between the poles and the tropics than there is now. Dinosaurs lived all over Earth, but so far, more fossils have been uncovered in America and China than in many other places.

155–145 MILLION YEARS AGO

Stegosaurus was the largest of the **stegosaurs**, a type of dinosaur found around the world. A plant-eating ornithischian, it could defend itself against predators with its clutch of tail spikes that is sometimes called a "thagomizer." The large plates on the back were well supplied with blood vessels and could possibly flush red, either as a warning or to attract a mate. They might have helped the dinosaur control its temperature, soaking up heat from sunlight or losing heat to a cooling wind.

Stegosaurus,
9 m (29.5 ft)

155 MILLION YEARS AGO

One species of
Diplodocus grew up to
32 m (110 ft) long.

154–152 MILLION YEARS AGO

Diplodocus, **one of the most famous of all dinosaurs**, was one of many large sauropods that roamed western North America. With animals such as *Diplodocus, Camarasaurus, Brontosaurus,* and *Apatosaurus* all living in the same area, they had different feeding strategies, revealed by their teeth. Their huge size kept them safe from predators as adults.

The Morrison Formation is an area rich in fossils from the period 156–147 million years ago. Stretching across the western United States and Canada, it's where some of the most famous dinosaurs lived. Excavations from the 1870s sparked public and scientific interest in dinosaurs. Fossils found there include *Gargoyleosaurus, Stegosaurus, Apatosaurus, Brontosaurus, Diplodocus, Camarasaurus, Allosaurus,* and *Torvosaurus.* The Morrison Formation covers 1.5 million square km (600,000 square miles), and only a fraction has been excavated—the rest is still buried.

154–150 MILLION YEARS AGO

Gargoyleosaurus was an **ankylosaur**, a type of heavy, squat dinosaur covered in bony armor—with a few spikes for good measure. Their protective covering made it hard for theropods to attack them as they moved slowly through the low-growing plants that they browsed.

Gargoyleosaurus,
3.5 m (11.5 ft)

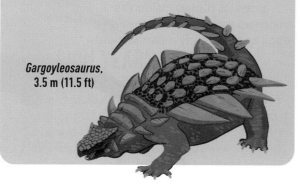

151 MILLION YEARS AGO

Not all theropods were huge. *Compsognathus* was a **much smaller theropod** that probably ate invertebrates and perhaps tiny or baby reptiles.

Compsognathus,
1 m (39 in) long

Pteradactylus,
1 m (39 in) wingspan

151–148.5 MILLION YEARS AGO

Pterodactylus was a **short-tailed pterosaur** that lived on the islands that made up Europe. Its teeth show that it was a meat eater and probably ate small invertebrates.

145 MILLION YEARS AGO

Early birds had claws on their wings and bones extending down the tail.

151–148.5 MILLION YEARS AGO

Birds evolved from small theropod dinosaurs in the late Jurassic and early Cretaceous. *Archaeopteryx* was on the **boundary between dinosaurs and birds**. It still had many features of dinosaurs that are not shared with modern birds, such as a long, bony tail, claws on its wings, and teeth in its beak. Yet, it was like birds in having feathers and being able to fly.

146 MILLION YEARS AGO

An **asteroid** 5–10 km (3–6 miles) across crashed into land that is now the Kalahari Desert in Africa, leaving a crater 75–80 km (46–50 miles) wide.

150 MILLION YEARS AGO

Insects that looked almost exactly like modern butterflies with "eyespots" on their wings, sipped nectar from early flowers and possibly helped pollinate plants. True butterflies evolved 50 million years later—these look-alikes were a type of **lacewing**.

145 MILLION YEARS AGO

At the end of the Jurassic and start of the Cretaceous periods, a series of **extinction events** stretched over 25 million years. During this time, there was a shift that saw the rapid evolution of birds and new variety in pterosaurs. Asteroid impacts and volcanic eruptions probably contributed to the extinctions.

GROWING ALIKE, GROWING APART

Some organisms that are unrelated to each other develop similar features in a process called convergent evolution. Other organisms start out the same but split into groups with features so different that they become different species.

GROWING ALIKE

Organisms evolve in response to challenges or pressures in their environment. The process is not deliberate or aiming at a goal, but when an organism appears that is well adapted to the conditions where it lives, it's more likely to survive and reproduce than one less well suited. Over time, the **features that work best for the organism become common in that species**. For example, animals that live in a snowy landscape often have white fur. This evolves over time since darker animals have a harder time stalking prey or hiding from predators. White animals are more likely to survive and breed, so they pass on the gene for white fur to future generations.

BEING STREAMLINED

In the same way, **animals that live in the water often develop a streamlined shape**. They arrive at this shape independently, just because it works best. This has happened over and over again. Ichthyosaurs and dolphins evolved shapes similar to those of fish. The Triassic reptile *Gulosaurus* developed a similar body shape, flippers, and tails to the marine mammal *Basilosaurus*, an early ancestor of whales, that lived 41–34 million years ago.

Gulosaurus, 1.5 m (5 ft) long, lived 250 million years ago and was a reptile.

Basilosaurus, 5–20 m (49–66 ft) long, lived 40 million years ago and was a mammal.

LAUNCHED!

Flying mammals have evolved **membranes of skin for gliding between trees** on several occasions. *Volaticotherium*, *Eomys*, and the modern sugar glider all fly in this way.

Eomys lived 25 million years ago.

Volaticotherium lived 164 million years ago.

GROWING APART

When South America and Africa separated, ancestors of elephants stranded on each side evolved into mastodons in South America and modern elephants in Africa.

The opposite of organisms coming to resemble others is organisms that **diverge** from their close relatives. This also happens because of environmental pressures. It drives **speciation**—new species splitting off from an existing species. It commonly happens when a group of organisms is separated from others of their kind, often by a geographical barrier, such as a mountain range or sea. As Pangea split apart, animals that had once been able to roam over a continuous landmass found themselves on a smaller block of land surrounded by sea, separated from other groups. When animals are split into separate living spaces, there might be different types of food available, different climates, different predators to escape from, and different environments in which to build a nest, burrow, or other living space. If different features or activities are better suited to one region than another, the animals start to differ. As time passes, they become increasingly different until they are distinct species.

PLATES AND SPINES

Stegosaurs (dinosaurs like *Stegosaurus*) probably first evolved in land that is now China. They spread around the world while the land in the north was still part of a single continent. Once the land split up, **stegosaurs in separate places evolved differently**. By the late Jurassic, different stegosaurs were spread widely. *Kentrosaurus* (152 million years ago) in Africa, *Stegosaurus* in North America (155–145 million years ago), *Dacentrus* (154–150 million years ago) in the UK, and *Tuojiangosaurus* (157–154 million years ago) in China were just a few of them.

Kentrosaurus, 4.5 m (15 ft) long, had large shoulder spikes and pointed plates on its back.

Stegosaurus, 9 m (29.5 ft) long, was larger but less spiky.

144–116 MILLION YEARS AGO

The Cretaceous, beginning about 144 million years ago, was a time of hot and cold periods. By 120 million years ago, the temperature had fallen far enough for ice to cover Antarctica. Pangea continued to break up, with the Atlantic Ocean opening between South America and Africa. Flowering plants and birds evolved on land, and the balance of life in the sea changed utterly, with bony fishes becoming common, and sharks and mosasaurs emerging as the top predators.

130–125 MILLION YEARS AGO

One of the first **flowering plants** (angiosperms) was *Montsechia*, which lived beneath the shallow waters of European lakes. Angiosperms next grew on land, becoming more common and numerous from around 113 million years ago. They soon spread around the world.

Marine algae called coccolithophores thrived during warm periods in the Jurassic and particularly the Cretaceous. Smaller than the width of a human hair, they served a vital function, producing oxygen and locking away carbon dioxide in the tiny shells they made from calcium carbonate. The famous White Cliffs of Dover in southern England are made of their shells, and the Cretaceous gets its name (which means "chalklike") from the rocks made of these shells. Coccolithophores are still with us.

Archaeofructus, an angiosperm from China, perhaps grew in the water 125 million years ago.

144 MILLION YEARS AGO

Baryonyx, 7.5–10 m (25–33 ft) long, was the first fish-eating dinosaur ever discovered.

130–125 MILLION YEARS AGO

Baryonyx was a theropod, but unlike others it had a **snout and teeth like a crocodile, nostrils a long way up its snout, and eyes high on its head**. These features suggest that it went in the water and ate fish. It probably spent a lot of time on land, too, and also ate small reptiles including young dinosaurs. It had a giant, hooked claw, 30 cm (12 in) long, which it might have used for hooking fish from the water as it stood on the bank.

130–122 MILLION YEARS AGO

The fossils of the **Jehol Biota** were laid down in parts of China. Fossil beds reveal a whole ecosystem with organisms including the earliest flowering plants, pterosaurs, feathered dinosaurs, mammals, early birds, insects, snails, spiders, turtles, amphibians, and fish. Dinosaurs found there include sauropods, theropods, and ankylosaurs.

129.4–122.5 MILLION YEARS AGO

Amargasaurus was not a typical sauropod. Shorter than most and with a shorter neck, it had **two rows of long spines** along its head and neck. The tallest were 60 cm (24 in) long. These might have been joined together by skin, making a kind of sail. Spikes could have deterred predators from attacking the animal or have been displayed to attract or warn off other *Amargasaurus*.

Amargasaurus, 9–10 m (30–33 ft) long

126–122 MILLION YEARS AGO

Iguanodon was one of a group of dinosaurs known as **iguandonts** found around the world. With a large thumb spike used to pull branches to its mouth, *Iguanodon* was a large plant-eater that probably lived in herds browsing vegetation. It was the second dinosaur to be discovered and named.

125–123 MILLION YEARS AGO

Sinodelphys, just 15 cm (6 in) long, lived in the trees of China where it probably ate insects and worms. It is the **earliest known marsupial**. Marsupials give birth to tiny, partly formed young, which then develop fully in a pouch on the mother's body, drinking milk she produces.

125–123 MILLION YEARS AGO

About the size of a badger, around 1 m (39 in) long, *Repenomamus* was the **only mammal known to have eaten dinosaurs**. A fossil of one was found with chunks of a *Psitticosaurus* inside its stomach!

124.6 MILLION YEARS AGO

Caudipteryx was a **feathered dinosaur** with long legs and a sharp, pointed beak. It could run fast, like a modern roadrunner, and had feathery plumes on its wings and tail, but it could not fly. Unusually for a theropod, it ate plants and seeds, but probably caught small animals or insects occasionally. It lived alongside other feathered dinosaurs.

Caudipteryx, 1 m (39 in) long, was on the boundary between dinosaur and bird.

116 MILLION YEARS AGO

126–101 MILLION YEARS AGO

Psittacosaurus was an early **ceratopsian**, like *Triceratops*. It had simple horny growths on the side of its head, but no frill. Its parrot-like beak could snip through plants or crush nuts and seeds. One fossil shows long bristles growing from the top of the tail. We don't know what *Psittacosaurus* used them for.

Many fossils of *Psittacosaurus* exist, suggesting that it was a common animal in China where it lived. It grew to 2 m (6.5 ft) long.

126–124 MILLION YEARS AGO

Fossils of many feathered dinosaurs have been found in China. They were all theropods, and most were quite small. One of these was *Sinosauropteryx*, the first **non-bird dinosaur with feathers** to be discovered. Chemicals preserved in the fossil show that it was patterned with dark and light feathers, with a striped tail.

Sinosauropteryx, 1 m (39 in) long

Ouranosaurus, 7–8.3 m (23–27 ft), had a toothless beak and a battery of chewing teeth at the back of its mouth.

125–113 MILLION YEARS AGO

Ouranosaurus was an African **ornithopod** with a large sail of skin and muscle on its back. Its mouth like a duck's bill was similar to those of hadrosaurs in North America.

FLYING WITH FEATHERS

Only one kind of dinosaur survived the catastrophic extinction event at the end of the Cretaceous, 65.5 million years ago. These were small, feathered theropods of a type called raptors or dromaeosaurids. Birds have evolved directly from them.

FROM DINOSAUR TO BIRD

Many fossils of **small, feathered dinosaurs** have been found in China, including one of the smallest dinosaurs, *Microraptor*. This had four wings—both its arms and legs had flight feathers. It still had a long tail with bones going all the way to the end and claws on its wings. Like *Archaeopteryx*, it lived on the boundary between bird and dinosaur. It isn't known whether it could fly by flapping its wings or if could only glide, perhaps after launching itself from a tree.

Microraptor lived around 125 million years ago, which is 25 million years later than *Archaeopteryx*.

Confuciusornis was a bit more **"bird."** It had a "pygostyle"—the part on a bird's rear where the flight feathers of the tail attach—but it doesn't seem to have had long tail feathers to help it fly. Instead, it had a bunch of shorter downy feathers and two long, streaming, ribbon-like feathers that might have served to attract a mate.

Confuciusornis, wingspan 70 cm (28 in), had feathers in gray, black, and either red or brown.

Scientists still argue about whether *Rahonavis*, which lived 70 million years ago, was a dinosaur or a bird and whether it could fly. It grew to 70 cm (28 in) long.

ALL TOGETHER

Birds didn't replace feathered dinosaurs. The two types of animal lived alongside each other until the other dinosaurs died out. In evolution, one type of organism—called a **"common ancestor"** by scientists—has descendants that take two or more separate paths. So one type of feathered dinosaur could have been the ancestor both to birds and to later feathered dinosaurs. Along one path, the animals lost the bone in their tails, the teeth in their beaks, and the claws on their wings to become the type of birds we recognize today. On the other path, they kept these features, never began to fly, and kept their reptilian lifestyles. The common ancestor had features that could evolve in either direction. When scientists try to figure out how organisms are related, they often look for features that a common ancestor would have had.

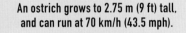

An ostrich grows to 2.75 m (9 ft) tall, and can run at 70 km/h (43.5 mph).

UN-BIRDING

Sometimes, evolution seems to go backward. A modern ostrich has feet that look very much like the feet of a theropod dinosaur. It can't fly, and it has few feathers on its neck, head, and legs. It looks more dinosaur than bird! *Hesperornis* was a **flightless bird** from the late Cretaceous. It had already given up flying and used its wings instead to help it swim through the water, as a modern penguin does.

Hesperornis, 1.8 m (6 ft) tall, lived 83.5–78 million years ago.

FEATHERS AND FLYING

Feathers and wings evolved long before birds could fly. Recent discoveries suggest that the earliest types of feathers might have appeared 250 million years ago on the ancestors of crocodiles, before dinosaurs and birds separated from a common ancestor with them. This is supported by the discovery that pterosaurs had fuzz, which might be related to feathers, and some dinosaurs that were not theropods seem to have had some form of feathers. Feathers probably helped keep animals warm, or helped them cover their eggs if they sat on a nest, or maybe allowed bright colors for displaying to possible mates.

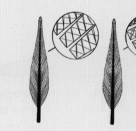

Feathers probably began as a single filament (thread), then a tuft of several filaments, later evolving into the separate barbs that hold modern feathers together.

80–65.5 MILLION YEARS AGO

India, previously an island, moved northward and began to collide with Asia at the end of the Cretaceous. An immediate effect was massive volcanic eruptions. The Deccan Traps poured out lava, covering much of India. These eruptions have sometimes been blamed for the extinction of the dinosaurs, and would certainly have had a huge impact on the climate.

75–71 MILLION YEARS AGO

Velociraptor was a small, speedy theropod that lived in Mongolia. It used the vicious claws on its hind legs to stab vital parts of its prey. Covered with feathers but unable to fly, *Velociraptor* was at least **partly warm-blooded**. Only warm-blooded animals need feathers or fur to keep their bodies warm, since they use energy to regulate their own temperature.

80 MILLION YEARS AGO

Elasmosaurus had a **longer neck** than any other plesiosaur. Its neck was stiff and moved mostly from side to side. *Elasmosaurus* probably approached a shoal of fish from beneath. Long, thin teeth protruding from the mouth meshed together, impaling and trapping prey. Its stiff flippers would have been useless for moving over land.

Elasmosaurus, 13–14 m (42.5–46 ft) long

80 MILLION YEARS AGO

76.7 MILLION YEARS AGO

The hadrosaur (duck-billed dinosaur) *Maiasaura* **cared for its young**. A fossilized nest site in North America preserves adults, young, and nests with eggs. The presence of young alongside the adults shows that the adults fed and cared for them after hatching.

Therizinosaurus grew to 9–10 m (30–33 ft) long and 4–5 m (13–16 ft) tall.

77–73.5 MILLION YEARS AGO

The hadrosaur *Parasaurolophus* had a **large, hollow crest on its head**. This was probably used for making deep calls to communicate with other *Parasaurolophus*. Males and females had slightly different crests, suggesting that they made different sounds.

Parasaurolophus, 9.5 m (31 ft) long

70 MILLION YEARS AGO

One of the most **bizarre dinosaurs** of all time, *Therizinosaurus* was large, possibly feathered, and had huge, scythe-like claws up to 1 m (39 in) long. Despite its fearsome looks, it probably ate plants, using its enormous claws to pull branches to its mouth.

Pachycephalosaurus,
4.5 m (15 ft) long

70–65.5 MILLION YEARS AGO

Pachycephalosaurus had a **thick, bony dome** on top of its head, which it probably bashed into the flanks of rivals in battles over mates or territory.

68–65.5 MILLION YEARS AGO

A stocky, armored dinosaur, *Ankylosaurus* cropped low-growing plants with its beak. Its heavy, wide body would have made it difficult for a predator to tip it over, and the top and sides were covered with bony plates and spikes. A huge **club at the end of the tail** was an extra defensive weapon, made of fused bony plates. It might have used this against predators, rival *Ankylosaurus*, or both.

Bones in the tail of *Ankylosaurus*, 6 m (20 ft) long, were fused into a stiff rod that helped swing the tail club.

65.5 MILLION YEARS AGO

68–65.5 MILLION YEARS AGO

Triceratops had a distinctive **neck frill and three horns**, probably used mostly for display, although it might have used them in tussles with other *Triceratops*. At least part of its body sprouted stiff bristles. It used its beak to pull branches to the chewing teeth at the back of its mouth.

Tyrannosaurus rex could grow to more than 12 m (39 ft) long, with a skull up to 1.5 m (5 ft) long.

68–65.5 MILLION YEARS AGO

The **most famous dinosaur of all**, *Tyrannosaurus rex*, lived right at the end of the age of dinosaurs. With teeth as long as a banana, it could eat other huge dinosaurs, such as *Triceratops*, *Ankylosaurus*, and hadrosaurs, as well as many smaller animals. *T. rex* probably killed its prey by biting into the neck or back.

Triceratops was 9 m (29.5 ft) long, and its skull could be nearly a third of its entire length.

Some of the most famous North American dinosaur fossils have been found in the Hell Creek Formation. Fossils laid down there at the end of the Cretaceous include *Ankylosaurus*, *Triceratops*, *T. rex*, and *Pachycephalosaurus*. It also preserves a huge number of plant fossils, including flowering plants such as early forms of magnolia and fruits, showing what the floodplain was like when dinosaurs lived there.

A SUDDEN END

The world of the dinosaurs came to an end in an instant. While most mass extinctions are spread over thousands or even hundreds of thousands of years, the catastrophe at the end of the Cretaceous, 65.5 million years ago, was caused by a huge asteroid (a rock from space) crashing into Earth. It happened one day in the northern hemisphere's spring. The effects were devastating and lasted for years.

IMPACT!

The **asteroid**, bigger than Mount Everest at around 10 km (6.2 miles) across, slammed into the coast of Mexico. After hurtling through space at 72,000 km/h (45,000 mph), it made a crater 180 km (112 miles) wide. A smaller chunk might have hit Africa at the same time. The energy of the crash was greater than a billion atomic bombs, and the asteroid instantly vaporized, turning to gas because it was so hot. The same happened to the rock and sea of the area it struck. A flash of heat spread outward, starting fires even long distances from the impact site.

CATASTROPHE

Every living thing within 1,450 km (900 miles) of the impact site was killed instantly. Huge tsunami (giant waves) nearly a mile high flooded far inland, destroying forests. Shockwaves passing through Earth caused catastrophic **earthquakes and tsunami** very far from the impact site. The air filled with blobs of molten rock hardening into pellets, poisonous gases, and soon with acidic rain. In the minutes and hours after the impact, it would have been dark and scorching hot in North America. Dinosaurs such as *Tyrannosaurus rex* and *Triceratops* were in the front line. Around the world, a rain of rock bombarded the land and heated the air, starting more fires. No region on Earth was safe.

FROM HOT TO COLD, THEN BACK TO HOT

The immediate firestorm gave way to years of **extreme cold**. The air was clogged with ash and dust that blocked the light and heat from the Sun, and the temperature fell. Even after the dust settled, chemicals remained in the air as aerosols (suspended droplets) that continued to block the Sun's heat and cool Earth. The average temperature plunged, dropping more than 25° C (45° F), so that even in the tropics it was only 5° C (41° F), and in most areas it was below freezing. The average global temperature remained below freezing for 3–16 years, and it took more than 30 years for the climate to recover. By then, it settled into a **hotter temperature** than before the impact, because the carbon dioxide added to the air by the disaster produced a greenhouse effect, trapping heat and making Earth hotter than before the disaster.

WORLD WITHOUT FOOD

The lack of light and heat **killed animals and plants**. As plants died, plant-eaters had nothing to eat, and they soon died, too. Meat-eaters ate their bodies for awhile, then they also ran out of food. In the oceans, currents and temperatures were disrupted. Plankton died, bringing down whole food chains. Around three-quarters of all species died. On land, these included the dinosaurs and pterosaurs. In the sea, the ammonites, plesiosaurs, and mosasaurs came to an end. It remained semidark all over Earth for around ten years. Only the small animals that could hide from danger, perhaps underground or in caves, and feed on the dead or seeds could survive. Seeds that lay buried in the ground did not sprout until the heat and light returned.

CHAPTER 5

MAMMALS TAKE OVER

The asteroid strike 65.5 million years ago laid waste to Earth, plunging it into darkness and a 10-year-long winter. Yet, not everything died. Enough plants and animals survived for life to recover. After soot finally stopped falling from the sky and sunlight broke through, the temperature rose and seeds germinated. The surviving animals—insects, some small mammals, crocodiles, turtles, snakes, birds, and a few others—came out of hiding and began to flourish again. With many living spaces left empty, there was plenty of land and sea for them to inhabit. Organisms spread, bred, adapted, and became more varied. It would take millions of years for Earth to return to anything like the variety it had before the deadly asteroid. Yet, life took off, and evolution rapidly began to fill the gaps left by non-bird dinosaurs, flying reptiles, and large marine reptiles. The only surviving dinosaurs, the birds, are still with us today. The tiny mammals that ran between the feet of the dinosaurs grew to dominate the planet. There are now 5,500 species of mammals on Earth, and we are one of them.

65.5–56 MILLION YEARS AGO

While North and South America were becoming joined on one side of the world, a few primates on the other side of the growing Atlantic were emerging from the trees. These early ancestors of humans were at first little different from any other animal of the forests and plains.

Some organisms that lived before the extinction event survived and flourished in a new, different world. In the seas, ray-finned fishes became the most common. Freshwater and marine turtles survived the extinction event well, as did amphibians.

The crocodile-like *Borealosuchus*, 2.8 m (9.2 ft) long, first appeared around 70 million years ago and survived until 48 million years ago.

The soft-shelled turtle *Axestemys* had leathery skin rather than a hard shell. From the late Cretaceous, it survived until 45 million years ago.

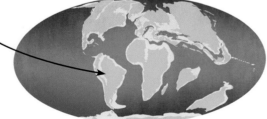

65.5 MILLION YEARS AGO

65.5 MILLION YEARS AGO

The **landmasses** were **not yet in their current positions**. North and South America were not yet connected, Australia was near Antarctica, and Europe was much closer to North America than it is now. This limited the movement of animals around the world. The average global temperature was much warmer than now at 24–25° C (75–77° F).

Positions of landmasses 65.5 million years ago

65 MILLION YEARS AGO—NOW

The **giant conifer** *Metasequoia* grew to 40 m (131 ft) tall.

62–55 MILLION YEARS AGO

One of the first **waterbirds**, *Presbyornis* was a giant goose-shaped bird with long legs. It lived in flocks, wading into lakes and rivers to filter food from the water with its beak.

Presbyornis, 1.5 m (5 ft)

65.5 MILLION YEARS AGO

Almost immediately after the extinction event, **ferns** began to grow again. Even now, they are one of the first plants to return after wildfires.

61.5—58 MILLION YEARS AGO

An early type of **penguin**, *Waimanu* looked like something between a penguin and a diving bird such as an auk or loon. Already it was flightless, with wings adapted for swimming.

Waimanu, 100 cm (39 in) tall

60 MILLION YEARS AGO

Earlier mammals had eaten invertebrates such as insects and worms, but now some began to eat other vertebrates. The first **carnivores** were ancestors of the cat, dog, weasel, and bear families.

59 MILLION YEARS AGO—NOW

Ray-finned fish became the most common type of fish in the sea, largely replacing lobe-finned fish.

The disk-shaped *Mene,* or "moon fish," appeared 59 million years ago.

56—48 MILLION YEARS AGO

Eohippus was an early **ungulate**, which means it had hooves on its feet. From these first ungulates, animals as different as horses and rhinoceroses have evolved. *Eohippus* browsed low-growing plants, but some early ungulates ate meat at least some of the time.

Eohippus, an early relative of the horse, stood 30 cm (12 in) to the shoulder.

56 MILLION YEARS AGO

60—58 MILLION YEARS AGO

The largest **snake** ever known, *Titanoboa*, lived in the tropical rain forests of South America, where it grew to 13 m (42.5 ft) long. It possibly ate crocodiles.

58—55 MILLION YEARS AGO

Plesiadapis was a small mammal with long fingers well suited to holding branches. It was possibly one of the earliest **primates** or at least related to them.

Plesiadapis, 80 cm (31.5 in)

56—34 MILLION YEARS AGO

Uintatherium was a **large, plant-eating ungulate** the size of a rhino. It probably used its large canine teeth to dig up roots or collect water plants. The inward-curving skull left little room for its brain, which was rather small.

The male *Uintatherium,* 4 m (13 ft) long, had three pairs of horns, probably used to attract a mate or fight with other males.

Gastornis might have weighed as much as an adult man.

56—45 MILLION YEARS AGO

The **giant flightless bird** *Gastornis* stood 2 m (6.6 ft) tall. Probably a plant-eater, it possibly cracked nuts like coconuts with its powerful beak.

MAMMALS CREEP FROM THE SHADOWS

Although the first mammals evolved in the Triassic, they stayed small during the reign of the dinosaurs. Most probably lived in trees, and many were nocturnal (active at night) when dinosaurs were not around. Living in burrows or trees would protect them from predators, and also from being stomped on by large feet! Mammals were one of the groups worst affected by the extinction event, with more than 90 percent of species dying. Yet with the dinosaurs gone, the survivors came out into the open. Over ten million years, they quickly diversified and grew much larger.

Today's diverse mammals evolved from the tiny mammals that survived the extinction event.

Modern elephants have only sparse bristles and live in hot places, but mammoths had a coat of fur to keep them warm in frozen landscapes.

BEING A MAMMAL

Mammals differ from the reptiles they evolved from in being **warm-blooded**, having **hair or fur**, giving birth to **live babies** (usually) and producing **milk** for their young. They also have a distinctive structure to the bones of their ears, which has developed from changes in the jaw.

Being warm-blooded means that an animal controls its own body temperature. A cold-blooded animal, such as a snake or turtle, needs to be warmed by the sun and is inactive when it's cold. These animals can't be nocturnal, since it's colder at night. Warm-blooded animals have hair or fur to insulate their bodies. Large mammals in warm climates have very little hair, because they would quickly get too hot—but being large and having hair means that a mammal can survive well even in extreme cold.

The first mammals **laid eggs**, and modern monotremes still do this. The **placental mammals**—which is now most mammals—grow their babies inside the mother's body. The baby is nourished through an organ called the placenta, which grows for that purpose and is lost when the baby is born. The mother produces milk to feed the baby after its birth. Even mammals that live underwater, like whales and dolphins, produce milk.

MAMMALIAN MEALS

The first mammals ate insects and other small invertebrates. As mammals grew larger, insects were no longer enough. By 60 million years ago, there were **herbivorous** (plant-eating) and **carnivorous** (meat-eating) mammals. Carnivores could eat reptiles, fish, amphibians, birds, and even other mammals. There were no large carnivores for a long time, and many carnivores were often scavengers, picking up dead animals rather than hunting prey.

Purgatorius, 15 cm (6 in) long, was an insect-eating mammal that lived in the trees 65–63 million years ago.

Ocepeia, 30–70 cm (12–28 in) long, lived 61–57 million years ago in Africa, where it ate leaves.

The change in the **teeth** of mammals between 65.5 and 60 million years ago shows their changing diet. Meat-eaters have sharp, pointed canine teeth for delivering a killing bite and cutting teeth for shearing meat from bone. Plant-eaters have teeth to suit how they eat. Some have blade-like teeth to nip off leaves or branches they swallow whole, while others have grinding teeth for chewing up tough vegetation. Some have teeth for gnawing and scraping.

Arctocyon, which lived 61–57 million years ago, was at least partly carnivorous. Slow and heavy, it could climb trees and probably relied on surprise to attack its prey.

IN THE WATER

Just as some reptiles had returned to live in the water, so some mammals took to the **seas**. The whales and dolphins alive today have their ancestors in the early protowhales like *Ambulocetus*, which lived 49–47 million years ago. These evolved from doglike animals that lived on land and in the water in Pakistan. Marine mammals still need to breathe air and must come to the surface to do so.

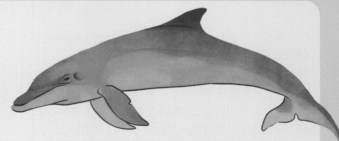

Although whales and dolphins don't look like most other mammals, they still breathe air and give birth to live young.

55–45 MILLION YEARS AGO

By 55 million years ago, the climate had warmed considerably. The start of this period saw the warmest five million years in the last 65 million years, with crocodiles in the Arctic and palm trees in Alaska. There were large rain forests with mangroves in Europe, extending as far as southern England, and trees even near the North Pole. Around the tropics, seawater was the temperature of a bath, at 35 °C (95 °F).

55 MILLION YEARS AGO

Mammal diversification produced the first rodents, rabbits, sirenians (animals like dugongs), horses, elephants, and armadillos.

52 MILLION YEARS AGO

The first eucalyptus (gum) trees grew in South America.

55 MILLION YEARS AGO

Phenacodus was an early **ungulate**. Although it had five toes, it put its weight mostly on the middle toes. Eventually, ungulates would lose the extra toes.

Phenacodus, 1.7 m (5.5 ft) long

55 MILLION YEARS AGO

55 MILLION YEARS AGO

Flowering plants **coevolved** with the animals that pollinated them. Many flowers are pollinated by insects and others by bats and birds.

55 MILLION YEARS AGO

Birds diversified into groups seen today, including songbirds, divers, parrots, swifts, and woodpeckers.

Icaronycteris, 14 cm (5.5 in) long, is the second-earliest bat known.

52 MILLION YEARS AGO

Icaronycteris was an early **bat that used echolocation**. Bats appeared at least 52.5 million years ago and possibly earlier, but their thin, fragile bones don't fossilize readily.

Coevolution happens when two organisms evolve together, forming a close relationship that benefits both and relies on particular features in each. For example, hummingbirds and the flowers they feed from have coevolved, with flowers producing nectar deep within the flower and the bird evolving a very long beak and tongue to reach it.

50–40 MILLION YEARS AGO

One of the first **camels** was *Protylopus*, which lived in North America. Although camels grew large later, *Protylopus* was about the size of a rabbit.

Pakicetus, 1–2 m (3.3–6.6 ft), had a long skull—still a characteristic of whales.

50 MILLION YEARS AGO

The first **tapirs** (related to rhinos) and **camels** appeared. Modern camels and camelids such as llamas and vicuña evolved from them. **Primates** also began to diversify around this time.

45 MILLION YEARS AGO

The first **butterflies** appeared. They have coevolved with flowering plants, since both the adults and young (caterpillars) rely on them for food.

50 MILLION YEARS AGO

Pakicetus is classed as the **first whale**, although it still lived on land. Looking somewhat like a wolf, it roamed the shores of the ocean eating small animals and fish before its descendants took to the sea.

45 MILLION YEARS AGO

49 MILLION YEARS AGO

A period of **global cooling** began, with a large drop in the level of carbon dioxide in the atmosphere. This was possibly caused by a large number of small water plants called *Azolla* growing in the warm waters of the Arctic, then dying and sinking to the seabed where the carbon they contained was locked away in sedimentary rock. This continued over around 800,000 years, starting the "ice house" (cold) period that continues today.

INDIA

49–47 MILLION YEARS AGO

An early **whale**, *Ambulocetus* probably spent a lot of time in the water like a modern hippo. Its sprawling legs would have made it slow and clumsy on land.

50 MILLION YEARS AGO

India, which had been an island in the southern hemisphere, finished moving northward and became part of Eurasia. Organisms from India mixed with those of Eurasia, and both had to get used to new predators, prey, and environments.

Ambulocetus, 3.5 m (11 ft) long, was at home in rivers and coastal waters.

44—35 MILLION YEARS AGO

As the climate became drier, the lush forests began to change. Evergreen trees were replaced by deciduous trees (those that lose their leaves in winter), which are better able to cope with changing temperatures. By the end of the period, only the tropics still had evergreen rain forests, and elsewhere vast forests of deciduous trees had spread.

43—41 MILLION YEARS AGO

Andrewsarchus is sometimes presented as a fierce predator, but we don't know for sure. Only the **skull** has been found. While that's large and could clearly give a powerful bite, it's possible that *Andrewsarchus* wandered the beaches crunching through shellfish and turtles rather than hunting large animals. It might have eaten carrion and maybe used its large teeth to grub up roots.

The skull of *Andrewsarchus* was 83 cm (33 in) long.

40—34 MILLION YEARS AGO

Basilosaurus was a **whale fully adapted to life in the water**, with its limbs shrunk to flippers useful only for swimming. It was one of the largest animals known between the extinction of the dinosaurs and the appearance of large modern whales around 15 million years ago.

Basilosaurus, 15—20 m (49—66 ft)

44 MILLION YEARS AGO

40 MILLION YEARS AGO

Rodents were carried on rafts of drifting vegetation, such as mangrove roots, from Africa to South America. The distance across the Atlantic Ocean was much shorter than it is now, since the continents have drifted farther apart—and are still moving. In their new land, some of the rodents evolved to be much larger and replaced some marsupials already living there. Modern porcupines and capybaras evolved from these early arrivals.

Hesperocyon, 80 cm (31.5 in)

40—31 MILLION YEARS AGO

Hesperocyon is the earliest known animal in the **dog family**, in a line that later gave rise to foxes, wolves, coyotes, jackals, and dogs. Slightly built, it probably looked more like a small raccoon or civet than a modern dog.

40 MILLION YEARS AGO

Horse-like mammals diversified quickly, their hooves changing as time passed. Their feet lost the outer toes, leaving the two parts of the hoof of a modern horse (see page 101).

Mesohippus was a horse 60 cm (24 in) tall that lived 40—30 million years ago in North America.

40 MILLION YEARS AGO

A group of small mammals that would give rise to bears, pandas, and raccoons evolved. The first identifiable **bear**, the "dawn bear," evolved 20 million years ago.

38–26 MILLION YEARS AGO

One of the earliest forms of **rhinoceros**, *Subhyracadon* resembled a modern rhino, but had no horns. It grew to around 2.4 m (8 ft) long and lived in North America.

37–35 MILLION YEARS AGO

Moeritherium was an early **relative of elephants** with a short trunk and small tusks. It lived like a modern hippopotamus, spending much of its time standing in water in the swamps of North Africa.

Moeritherium,
2.4 m (8 ft) long

35 MILLION YEARS AGO

Megacerops was 5 m (16.4 ft) long and 2.5 m (8 ft) tall to the shoulder.

36 MILLION YEARS AGO

"Old World" **primates** (those from Africa) arrived in South America, carried on rafts of floating vegetation across the sea. They dispersed and diversified in South America, producing all the lines of "New World" (South American) monkeys.

Monkeys on a floating raft of vegetation

38–34 MILLION YEARS AGO

Living on the plains of North America, *Megacerops* looked like a rhinoceros with extra horns, but was not related to rhinos. One of the **largest animals of its time**, it was too big for any predator to tackle. It browsed low-growing plants. It was not adapted to eating grass and died out as its habitat changed to grasslands and the food it needed disappeared.

Baleen

Whale with baleen

Toothed whale

35 MILLION YEARS AGO

Whales divided into two groups: those that had **baleen** and filtered food from the seawater, and **toothed whales**, which could bite larger prey. Baleen hangs as a curtain of bristle-like material inside the whale's mouth. The whale takes in a mouthful of water and then forces it out through the baleen, trapping small organisms in its mouth.

34–24 MILLION YEARS AGO

The world was cold 34 million years ago. Lasting ice sheets had formed in Antarctica for the first time in half a billion years (and are still there). So much water was locked up in ice that sea levels were 105 m (344 ft) lower than now, and some land that had been below the sea became dry. Africa moved northward to collide with Europe, pushing up the Alps, while the Himalayas continued to grow as India pushed against Asia. The first deer evolved in these new mountain habitats.

34 MILLION YEARS AGO

The first **hummingbirds** appeared. With a long beak and the ability to hover by flapping their wings extremely fast, they are perfectly adapted to taking nectar from flowers on the wing.

33–23 MILLION YEARS AGO

Paraceratherium was the **largest-ever terrestrial mammal**. A plant-eater that lived in Asia, it was tall enough to reach leaves that grew too high for other animals. It was probably as large as a land mammal can grow. Warm-blooded animals produce heat constantly and would have difficulty keeping cool enough if they grew larger.

At 7.4 m (24 ft) long and 4.8 m (15.5 ft) tall at the shoulder, *Paraceratherium* was much bigger than an elephant.

34 MILLION YEARS AGO

34 MILLION YEARS AGO

Eomys was a **gliding rodent**, with flaps of skin stretched between its front and rear legs. It could use these to glide between trees.

Eomys, 25 cm (10 in)

30–28 MILLION YEARS AGO

Apidium was an early **monkey** that lived in North Africa. With hands adapted to grasping branches, it lived in the trees, eating fruit and insects.

Apidium, 30 cm (12 in) excluding tail

33 MILLION YEARS AGO

The **sea eagle** *Haliaeetus* first appeared, one of the oldest surviving groups of bird.

32.5 MILLION YEARS AGO

The first **grasslands** appeared in Chile 15 million years before they spread elsewhere. At first, rodents ate the grass and its seeds, but later large grazers evolved to take advantage of this new ecosystem.

30 MILLION YEARS AGO

Stenomylus was a tiny early **camel** that lived in North America. This slender, humpless camel seems to have lived in large herds; many fossils have been found together.

Stenomylus, 60 cm (12 in) tall

25–2.5 MILLION YEARS AGO

Pelagornis was the **largest bird ever to fly**. A coastal bird, it fed on fish. The beak had "pseudoteeth," which were hollow spikes that were part of the jawbone itself, not separate teeth rooted in the jaw. Birds with true teeth have not existed since the death of the non-bird dinosaurs.

Pelagornis had a wingspan of 6–7.4 m (20–24 ft).

24 MILLION YEARS AGO

32.5 MILLION YEARS AGO

The first type of **chinchilla**, with teeth adapted to eating grass, lived in the early grasslands of Chile.

28 MILLION–3,000 YEARS AGO

Mekosuchus was a **crocodile** that climbed trees in Australia.

30 MILLION YEARS AGO

The **closing of the sea** between Asia and Eurasia led to animals moving between the two areas and mixing. Some European animals were driven to extinction by new predators or competitors for food and living spaces.

The size of *Branisella* is unknown as only the skull survives.

26 MILLION YEARS AGO

Branisella is the oldest **New World (South American) monkey**. It might have crossed from Africa, or it could have been a descendant of the monkeys that made the crossing.

24–22 MILLION YEARS AGO

Enaliarctos is the earliest known **seal**. It evolved from land-going mammals that returned to the sea. While modern seals swim using only their rear legs, and sea lions swim using only their front legs, *Enaliarctos* swam using all four limbs.

Enaliarctos, 1.5 m (6 ft) long

GRASSLANDS AND GRAZERS

Falling temperatures and drier conditions led to grass taking over many areas that had been forested. At first, grass grew only along the banks of rivers, but as conditions changed it spread to make vast, open plains. Animals followed, evolving to make the most of this new type of food and new habitat.

A SLOW START

Grasses first evolved 60–55 million years ago as just another of many types of plants. Grass can cope with lower levels of carbon dioxide than many plants, and as carbon dioxide levels and temperatures fell, forests died out, allowing grasslands to spread.

NEW TEETH FOR NEW PLANTS

At first, only rodents ate the grass, but over time browsers adapted to eat it. Grass is hard on animals' **teeth**. It is tough, dry, and contains tiny, hard particles of minerals it takes from the soil. To eat grass, an animal must put its mouth to the ground, often taking in some soil, which is also hard on teeth. Teeth changed to cope with eating grass. The teeth of large grazers—called "hypsodont" teeth—became very tall with thick enamel which was protection against being worn down by eating grass.

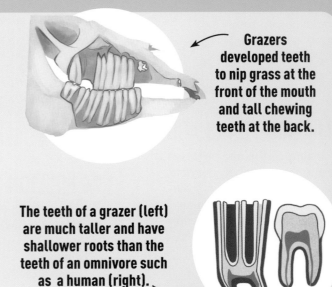

Grazers developed teeth to nip grass at the front of the mouth and tall chewing teeth at the back.

The teeth of a grazer (left) are much taller and have shallower roots than the teeth of an omnivore such as a human (right).

GRAZING AS A NEW LIFESTYLE CHOICE

Some grazers grew very large. There are still large grazers now, such as cows and hippos. Others were smaller and more nimble. The **horses** evolved to eat grass, starting small. The early horse *Merychippus*, at 90 cm (36 in) tall, was the tallest horse of its time.

Although grazers ate the grass, they helped it, too. Grass is not killed by being cropped. It can afford to lose its leaves to grazers because it grows up again from just above the root. This growing part is not eaten by grazers. While the grazers eat the grass, they also trample or eat saplings and other plants that compete with it.

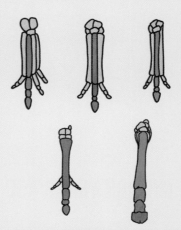

Teleoceras, 3 m (10 ft) long, weighed about 1,800 kg (4,000 lb). It lived in North America 16–5 million years ago.

The early horse *Merychippus* lived in North America 17–10 million years ago.

FOOTFALL

The change from forest to grassland wasn't just a switch from one type of plant to another: It had other effects. A forest floor is covered with rotting vegetation. It's generally soft and wet. A forest is dark, or dappled, and it's quite easy to hide in, either from predators or from prey. A grassy plain has hard, dry ground with no hiding places beyond the grass itself. Many grazers evolved a new type of **foot**, and long, slender legs adapted for running from danger.

A horse's foot now has a single **hoof**, but it has evolved from a foot with four toes. *Eohippus* put its weight on one of four toes, the other three becoming shorter and eventually, over millions of years, disappearing. The hoof has no squashy pad underneath and can afford to be narrow as there is no danger of sinking into soft ground in dry grassland. The hard, small hoof on a long leg enabled horses to run fast and escape from predators.

The reducing toes of grazers (left to right), ending with a hoof (bottom right), show how animals adapted to a new landscape.

NEW HOMES

The grasslands were not only home to grazers and their predators. They provided a new **underground habitat**, free of large tree roots, for animals such as the burrowing *Palaeocastor*. And some primates, ancestors of humans, left the trees and **walked upright,** so that they could see over the tall grasses.

The early beaver *Palaeocastor* built spiral burrows beneath the grasslands.

23–11 MILLION YEARS AGO

By 23 million years ago, most families of modern mammals had appeared, although the animals did not look like they do now. As grasslands replaced forest, grazing animals grew more diverse, with camels, pigs, deer, horses, and rhinos evolving. North and South America were still separated, with different animals living on each continent.

23 MILLION YEARS AGO

Large undersea forests of **kelp** grew, supporting a range of animals, from mammals such as *Enaliarctos* to shellfish. A type of large alga, modern kelp can grow to 45 m (150 ft). Kelp are fixed to the seabed with a "holdfast" and grow straight upward.

Kelp photosynthesizes, producing valuable oxygen. Gas bladders on the leaflike blades help keep them directed toward the surface and sunlight.

20.4–13.6 MILLION YEARS AGO

Tomarctus was a **dog** with bone-crushing jaws like a hyena. It lived in North America where it scavenged dead animals and probably also hunted prey.

23 MILLION YEARS AGO

21 MILLION YEARS AGO

The forests of North America started to die, and grass moved in, eventually forming **vast plains** that supported many grazers and the carnivores that preyed on them.

20.6–5 MILLION YEARS AGO

Giant camels such as *Hesperocamelus* and *Aepycamelus* were found coast to coast in central North America. They grew very tall and lived like giraffes do now, browsing on the leaves of trees.

Aepycamelus, 3 m (10 ft) tall, or 3.2 m (10.5 ft) long

20–3.6 MILLION YEARS AGO

Megalodon was the **largest shark that ever lived**, three times as long as the largest great white shark. Its size has been calculated from the size of its teeth, which can be up to 18 cm (7 in) long. It could have eaten almost anything else in the sea, including whales.

Megalodon probably grew to 15–18 m (49–59 ft) long, but no complete skeleton has been found.

20 MILLION YEARS AGO

Tiny coral polyps began to build what is now the **Great Barrier Reef** off the coast of Australia. Corals of different types had evolved and gone extinct several times over 500 million years. Their last extinction was around 40 million years ago, caused by global warming.

20–13 MILLION YEARS AGO

The giant **"terror bird"** *Phorusrhacos* lived in South America, where it was the top predator. It could run very fast, and with its clawed wings and huge, hook-tipped beak, it could easily catch and eat small mammals.

Phorusrhacos, 2.5 m (8.2 ft) tall

20–2 MILLION YEARS AGO

Deinotherium was **distantly related to modern elephants**, but not a direct ancestor of them. It had a trunklike nose and small downward-pointing tusks. The only land mammal to grow larger was *Paraceratherium* (see page 98). While modern elephants grow tusks from the upper jaw, *Deinotherium*'s tusks grew from the lower jaw. It's not known how it used them.

Deinotherium, 4 m (13 ft) tall at the shoulder

11 MILLION YEARS AGO

Xiphiacetus, 2 m (6.5 ft) long

20–7 MILLION YEARS AGO

The dolphin-like *Xiphiacetus* probably used **echolocation** as modern dolphins do—making clicking noises and listening for the echo to judge where objects are. It possibly swiped its long upper jaw at shoals of fish, then ate the injured or stunned ones.

13–12 MILLION YEARS AGO

The **giant whale** *Livyatan* had the longest teeth of any animal at 35 cm (13.7 in). Its 3 m (10 ft) skull is the only part that survives. It lived alongside *Megalodon* and ate the same animals, including smaller whales.

Livyatan, 13.5–17.5 m (44–57 ft) long

Chalicotherium, 2.6 m (8 ft) tall at the shoulder

16–3.6 MILLION YEARS AGO

Like a **cross between a horse and sloth**, *Chalicotherium* was a huge, plant-eating mammal that walked on its hind legs and knuckles. The hands had very long claws, which it used to pull branches to its mouth to feed on leaves. It held its fingers bent as it walked to protect the claws.

10–3 MILLION YEARS AGO

Plant-eating animals like *Deinotherium* and *Chalicotherium* grew to enormous sizes, and biologists call them "megafauna" (which just means "very big animals"). They needed to eat a huge quantity of plant matter to keep their bodies going and needed an enormous gut to process it. As grasses evolved to become tougher and harder for animals to process, many of these megafauna died out. Over the last 10 million years, six of the 24 main groups of earlier mammals have died out.

10 MILLION–30,000 YEARS AGO

The **giant camel** *Titanotylopus* moved from North America to Eurasia, crossing the land bridge at the Bering Straits (between Alaska and eastern Russia). Asian and African camels evolved from this, surviving after camels died out in North America.

Thylacosmilus, 1.2 m (4 ft) long

9–3 MILLION YEARS AGO

Thylacosmilus was a large, predatory **marsupial with saber teeth**. As a marsupial, the mother carried the babies around in a pouch. *Thylacosmilus* lived in South America.

10 MILLION YEARS AGO

Deinogalerix, 30–60 cm (12–24 in) long, had fur rather than spines and looked more like a rat than a hedgehog.

9–6.8 MILLION YEARS AGO

The **giant bird** *Argentavis* had a wingspan of up to 6.5 m (21 ft)—the size of a small plane. The only larger known bird was *Pelagornis*, which lived in North America 25 million years ago (see page 99). *Argentavis* might have been an active hunter, or perhaps more often ate carrion (dead meat).

Argentavis preying on *Macroeuphractus*

9–3 MILLION YEARS AGO

Macroeuphractus was a **giant carnivorous armadillo** around 1 m (39 in long). It lived in the grasslands of South America, where it might have been eaten by huge birds such as *Argentavis* and terror birds like *Phorusrhacos*.

10–7 MILLION YEARS AGO

Deinogalerix was a large, spineless **hedgehog** that lived in Italy.

9–7 MILLION YEARS AGO

Phoberomys was a huge, plant-eating South American **rodent** that looked similar to a guinea pig and grew to the size of a buffalo. The only rodent to grow larger was *Josephoartigasia*, which lived 4–2 million years ago.

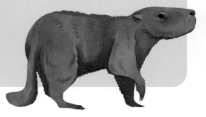

Josephoartigasia grew to 3 m (10 ft) long and weighed up to 1,000 kg (2,200 lb).

Phoberomys,
2.5–3 m (8–10 ft)

7 MILLION YEARS AGO

The giant, llama-like *Macrauchenia* lived in South America, where it ate plants. It probably belonged to the same family as modern tapirs, horses, and rhinos, a group called **perissodactyls**. This group's ancestors emerged 55 million years ago and eventually spread across much of the world.

Macrauchenia,
3 m (10 ft) long

5–2 MILLION YEARS AGO

The "bear otter" *Enhydriodon* was possibly the **first animal driven to extinction by hominins** (primates of the human family).

3 MILLION YEARS AGO

6 MILLION YEARS AGO

The entrance to the Mediterranean Sea from the Atlantic became sealed off, and the water in the sea evaporated, leading to a crisis for marine life. It was finally replaced by dry land covered in grass. The land connecting Europe and Africa allowed animals to **move between the two continents**.

5.3 MILLION YEARS AGO

The Zanclean Flood refilled the Mediterranean basin, creating the **Mediterranean Sea** in its current form. Water poured in from the Atlantic Ocean, raising the sea level as much as 10 m (33 ft) a day. It took between a few months and two years to fill.

4.2–1.9 MILLION YEARS AGO

Australopithecus was an early **hominin** and possibly the first humanlike primate to start using tools (see page 107).

5.3 MILLION–11,000 YEARS AGO

Mastodon was a large early **elephant** that roamed North and Central America, browsing and grazing. Other elephant-like animals included *Cuvieronius* in South America and the mammoths. Mammoths first appeared in Africa and moved into the Americas around 600,000 years ago.

5 MILLION YEARS AGO

The first **tree sloths and hippos** appeared, and also the giant ground sloth, *Megatherium*, in South America. There was even a seagoing sloth, *Thalassocnus*, which ate seaweed and seagrasses in shallow water.

Megatherium grew to the size of an elephant and lived until 80,000 years ago.

3.6 MILLION–10,000 YEARS AGO

Woolly rhinos emerged in cold places, starting in a mountainous plateau in Asia. Their range expanded as Earth grew colder in the last glacial period, which started 115,000 years ago.

OUT OF THE TREES

Humans are primates and belong to the same family as other apes (such as gorillas and chimpanzees). Monkeys are also primates, as are lemurs and tarsiers. The primate line split to give very different animals, found around the world and living in different ways. The path to the first humanlike primates such as *Australopithecus* took our ancestors from the trees to the plains and from being nocturnal to being active in daytime.

PRIMARY PRIMATES

The **very first primates** looked nothing like us. They were small animals that lived in the trees from around 55 million years ago. *Plesiadapis* (58–55 million years ago) was possibly not a primate itself, but was at least related to the first primates. It probably lived in trees eating insects and perhaps fruit. It has been found in Europe and North America, and it probably crossed using a land bridge linked to Greenland.

The **earliest known true primate** was *Archicebus*, which lived in China 55 million years ago. It weighed just 20–30 g (1 oz) and was smaller than the smallest living primate today, the pygmy lemur. It was possibly close to the point when animals like tarsiers split from the line that became apes.

Plesiadapis

Archicebus

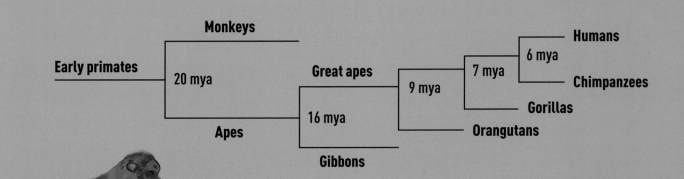

Early primates		Monkeys					Humans
	20 mya			Great apes		7 mya	6 mya
					9 mya		Chimpanzees
		Apes	16 mya				Gorillas
				Gibbons		Orangutans	

OVER THE SEA

The Old World primate *Aegyptopithecus* lived 33–29.5 million years ago in Egypt, which was wet and heavily forested. It probably lived in the trees and ate fruit.

Primates split first into two groups known as **wet-nosed primates and dry-nosed primates**. We belong to the dry-nosed primates, along with other apes, monkeys, and lemurs. The wet-nosed group now includes lemurs, bushbabies, and lorises. The dry-nosed primates split again into **tarsiers and simians** around 43 million years ago. Simians include all monkeys and apes. About 40 million years ago, some simians crossed the Atlantic Ocean and began to live in South America. All the **New World monkeys** evolved from them. All New World monkeys have tails, and some have prehensile tails—tails that they can use like an extra limb to hold onto tree branches and that can support their weight.

TAILLESS

Around 20 million years ago, the **monkeys and apes went their separate ways**. Apes became larger and had bigger brains, and they lost their tails. They could still live in the trees, swinging from branches, but some took to spending time on the ground, too.

The primate *Proconsul*, 1–1.5 m (3–5 ft) tall, lived 21–14 million years ago. Like later apes, it had no tail, but unlike them it moved mostly over the branches and could not easily swing from them.

IN THE GRASS

As grasslands became common, **some apes spent more time on the ground**. Beginning to walk or stand upright some of the time would have allowed them to look over the grass and perhaps spot any predators or other dangers well in advance. Around 12–10 million years ago, *Sivapithecus* in Thailand seems to have come down from the trees to live on the ground. Probably an ancestor of today's orangutans, *Sivapithecus* had teeth adapted to eating tough tubers. It could only have gathered these while on the ground.

Gigantopithecus was probably the largest ever ape, but its exact size is not known as there are few remains. It lived 2 million to 300,000 years ago in China.

TOWARD HUMANITY

From 9 million years ago, the lines of the current great apes began to separate. Our nearest relative in this line is the chimpanzee. We last shared an ancestor about 6 million years ago, and from there we can begin to trace our own uniquely **human line of ancestors**. One might have been *Ardipithecus*, which evolved in East Africa and spread throughout the continent. It was well adapted to going on two legs, but also still climbed trees. Our own family, *Homo*, emerged from a group of *Australopithecus*, which lived from 4.5 million years ago. Although *Australopithecus* was not yet human— not called *Homo*—it walked upright and probably used tools. It was on the way to becoming human.

Ardipithecus

Australopithecus

CHAPTER 6

A WORLD OF CHANGE

The last three million years have seen Earth settle into its current state, with its present arrangement of land and sea and today's climate. The biggest change to the land was North and South America joining together with a land bridge that is now Panama. Other changes that were already happening continued. The Atlantic Ocean has grown wider and still grows at about the same rate as your fingernails grow. The climate has seen warmer and cooler and colder periods, but it has stayed within a few degrees of current conditions. There have been ice caps at the poles throughout the period. It is in this world that humankind and the organisms that we depend on have developed. Since the rise of humans, Earth and its living things have changed faster than ever before. Humans have had a direct and massive impact on the plants, animals, and other organisms of the planet, and they continue to do so.

ON THE MOVE

Until 3.1 million years ago, the continents of North and South America were separated by sea, so most animals could not cross from one landmass to another. The land had split apart in the breakup of Pangea around 200 million years ago, so organisms had evolved independently in the two areas.

As the Americas and Africa moved farther apart, South America moved up to join North America.

ISLAND-HOPPING AND BRIDGE-BUILDING

Some animals **moved between North and South America** as islands emerged and disappeared in the sea between the lands, which was the result of rising and falling sea levels starting 12 million years ago. The first to move from North to South America included raccoon-like animals, small rodents like voles and lemmings, and a bit later, peccaries (in the pig family). Eventually, around 2.7 million years ago, the two landmasses were joined together by a **permanent bridge**. At this point, all types of animals could move between the continents, and they soon did so.

CREATURES OF NORTH AND SOUTH

The animals of North America had evolved with **links to Europe** through a land bridge at Greenland and sometimes through one connecting Alaska to eastern Russia. The animals of the north included ungulates and other browsers and grazers, but also fierce predators such as *Smilodon*.

South America had separated from North America before the evolution of predatory placental mammals. Since the area had once been linked with **Australia** through Antarctica, some of its animals were related to those of Australia, including marsupials (mammals that give birth to underdeveloped young that then live in a pouch on the mother's body). But the continent had been an island for around 50 million years. The role of large predators was filled in South America by giant snakes such as *Titanoboa*, fierce terror birds, and crocodiles.

ALL CHANGE

The **Great American Biotic Interchange** (GABI) is the name that scientists give the movement of animals between North and South America. From the north, animals including mammoths, horses, deer, rabbits, wolves, and cats moved south. From the south, glyptodons and other relatives of armadillos, sloths, large rodents, and huge, flightless terror birds moved north. Some doubtless fell prey to unfamiliar predators or could not compete successfully for food or living spaces, but overall most species survived the move.

The terror bird *Titanis* lived 5–1.8 million years ago. It was possibly outcompeted by northern predators such as *Smilodon*.

The ground sloth *Nothrotheriops*, 2.75 m (9 ft) long, evolved in North America and lived in Mexico and Texas until 11,000 years ago.

SUCCESSES AND FAILURES

Animals moving from North America to South America spread out in their new habitats. Those from the north seem to have spread out most successfully. Even so, the **ground sloths** successfully moved north, settling and further evolving in both continents. These huge animals had long, strong claws that—along with their size—probably protected them from the northern predators. The largest ground sloth could grow to 6 m (20 ft) long.

OCEAN EELS

Joining North and South America had another effect—it separated the Atlantic and Pacific Oceans, making it much harder for animals in one ocean to reach the other. One impact of this was the evolution of two different types of **eels** as the Pacific and Atlantic eels were forced to evolve in isolation.

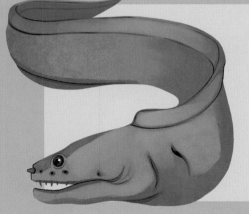

3–1 MILLION YEARS AGO

While North and South America were becoming joined on one side of the world, a few primates on the other side of the Atlantic were emerging from the trees. These early ancestors of humans were at first little different from any other animal of the forests and plains.

2.58 MILLION YEARS AGO

The latest **glaciation** (icy period) began, with the ice cap in the Arctic forming.

3 MILLION YEARS AGO—NOW

The first **swordfish** appeared, using their long, pointed bills to swipe and slash at the fish they ate. A similar style of fish had lived 100 million years ago—an example of convergent evolution, with similar features evolving separately.

2.5 MILLION–11,000 YEARS AGO

Glyptodon was a giant **armored mammal** that lived in swampy areas of South America. Similar to modern armadillos, but with a solid rather than jointed shell, it could draw its head in for protection against predators.

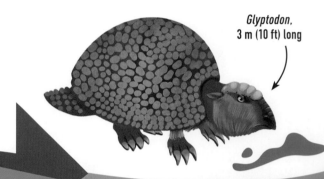

Glyptodon,
3 m (10 ft) long

3 MILLION YEARS AGO

2.8–1.5 MILLION YEARS AGO

One of the first of the **human** (*Homo*) species, *Homo habilis*, lived in Africa. They probably made the first stone tools. The first evidence of butchery (cutting up meat) is marks on animal bones from stone tools made 2.6 million years ago.

Homo habilis already looked recognizably human.

2.5 MILLION–4,000 YEARS AGO

The giant, ox-like *Pelorovis* was probably prevented from moving through forests by its **horns** more than 1 m (39 in) long. It lived in the grasslands of Africa.

2.6–0.6 MILLION YEARS AGO

Paranthropus was an early **hominin** that lived at the same time as some early human species. They used bone tools and possibly fire.

Paranthropus males grew to 132 cm (4 ft 6 in) and females to only 110 cm (3 ft 7 in), much smaller than modern humans.

Pelorovis,
3 m (10 ft) long

2.5 MILLION–10,000 YEARS AGO

The **sabertoothed cat** *Smilodon* was a top predator in both North and South America. It had teeth nearly 30 cm (1 ft) long, but a weak bite. *Smilodon* ate large herbivores such as bison.

Smilodon, 1.5 m (5 ft) long

People in China made carefully shaped stone tools like this hand ax.

2.1 MILLION YEARS AGO

Early humans began to live in grasslands rather than forests. They used **simple stone tools** to hunt and butcher grazing animals, including zebra and antelope.

1.8 MILLION–33,000 YEARS AGO

The **Steppe mammoth** appeared in Siberia. The ancestor of the woolly mammoth, some moved from Asia into North America by crossing the Bering land bridge 1.5 million years ago.

1.6 MILLION–44,000 YEARS AGO

Diprotodon, a **wombat** the size of a hippo, lived in Australia. The largest-ever marsupial, it ate only plants. Young *Diprotodon* were preyed on by marsupial lions.

1 MILLION YEARS AGO

1.9 MILLION YEARS AGO

The most recent type of **carnivorous plant** evolved, a carnivorous bromeliad. Carnivorous plants take some of their nourishment from trapping and consuming animals (usually insects). "Eating" has evolved independently in plants at least six times, starting nearly 86 million years ago.

2 MILLION YEARS AGO

The largest monotreme (egg-laying mammal) ever known was a **giant echidna**, *Murrayglossus*, that lived in Australia. It was 1 m (3.3 ft) long.

Arctotherium reached 4.3 m (14 ft) standing on its hind legs.

2 MILLION–40,000 YEARS AGO

Thylacoleo, or the **"pouch lion,"** was an Australian marsupial lion. It was the main predator of its time.

1.2 MILLION–11,000 YEARS AGO

Arctotherium was a **giant bear** in South America. It evolved from bears that moved south in the Great American Biotic Interchange. Despite its size, it probably wasn't a killer. Its short snout and very strong bite were suited to scavenging, including cracking open bones.

OUT OF AFRICA

Humans evolved in Africa, first in the forests and then in the grasslands. They didn't stay in Africa, though. Some species of humans moved in waves into Asia and Europe even before modern humans—*Homo sapiens*—evolved.

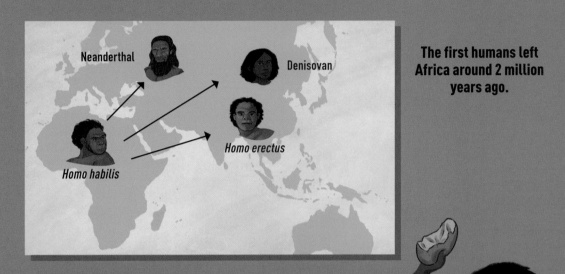

Neanderthal

Denisovan

Homo erectus

Homo habilis

The first humans left Africa around 2 million years ago.

FIRST HUMANS

The first humans known to **use tools** were *Homo habilis*, who lived in Africa. They were probably the first to make stone tools, which enabled them to cut meat they could not bite through, to break bones to reach the nutritious marrow, and to hunt animals they could not kill with their bare hands. Humans might have begun to control fire 2–1.7 million years ago and certainly by 1 million years ago. These were advantages that no other animal had ever had. It was the beginning of humankind having a huge effect on the environment and other organisms in it.

Homo habilis **using a pebble tool.**

FAR AFIELD

The first human species to **spread far beyond Africa** was *Homo erectus*. They reached China 2.12 million years ago and spread into the Middle East 1.8 million years ago. *Homo erectus* had bodies similar to modern humans. Their body hair might have been thinning, they had longer legs, smaller teeth, and larger brains than other apes. Brain size sets humans apart from other animals and has given us the ability to use tools and language.

Homo erectus **scraping an animal's skin with a hand ax.**

CONQUERING COLD

As humans spread, their bodies adapted to new environments, producing new species of human. **Using fire** to keep warm and making simple clothes from the skins of animals they killed, humans could move into areas that would otherwise be too cold for them to survive. Other animals had to evolve thicker fur and layers of fat to move into cold regions, which took thousands of years. Humans, though, could spread quickly. They entered areas as a new predator that other animals were not prepared for and could not adapt to quickly.

Homo erectus **was probably the first type of human to control fire consistently, around 1 million years ago.**

Homo heidelbergensis **might have been a common ancestor to several types of later humans, including ourselves.**

A SHARED ANCESTOR

Modern humans probably evolved in Africa around 315,000 years ago from a species called *Homo heidelbergensis*, which lived about 700,000–200,000 years ago. It's possible they were also the ancestors of Neanderthals and Denisovans, which evolved in other parts of the world.

LEAVING AFRICA AGAIN

When *Homo sapiens* left Africa to settle around the world, they were often entering places where earlier types of humans had already settled and made their lives. In Asia, they encountered **Denisovans**, and in Europe they met and lived alongside **Neanderthals**.

Human activities aren't unique to us. Neanderthals had bone and stone tools, used fire, created art, and probably had language and some type of spiritual life, because they buried their dead. Modern humans lived alongside these other types of humans but interbred with them, making families of mixed human types. We still have the DNA (genetic material) of some of these early humans in our bodies today.

1 MILLION–300,000 YEARS AGO

The last million years are the brief time in which humans have become the dominant species on the planet, with a huge impact on other organisms and the environment. Most of that impact has come in the last 10,000 years, but even earlier humans than *Homo sapiens* were shaping the world around them. Many of the animals that have lived over the last million years are still with us, although changing climate and human activity have brought some to extinction.

1 MILLION YEARS AGO

The modern **coyote** appeared, smaller than its ancestors. The coyote survives alongside its relatives, dogs and wolves, by eating a greater variety of food, including some carrion (animals it found already dead) and fruit.

Coyote, 1.3 m (4.3 ft) long

600,000–12,000 YEARS AGO

The European **cave lion** was one of the largest types of lion ever to live. It preyed on the megafauna of northern Europe, Asia, and America, tackling even cave bears and mammoths.

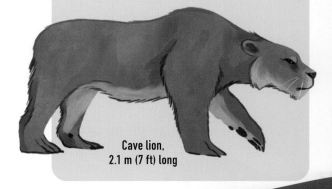

Cave lion, 2.1 m (7 ft) long

1 MILLION YEARS AGO

780,000–500,000 YEARS AGO

The climate warmed, bringing frost-free winters to Europe. **Giant hippos** lived in southern England; they were one and a half times the size of modern hippos.

500,000 YEARS AGO

The early human species *Homo heidelbergensis* probably started to use **hafted weapons** (those with a sharp point or blade attached to a shaft or handle).

Hafted weapons allowed humans to attack large animals from a safe distance.

New species can evolve if a group of organisms is stranded in an area where conditions are different or become different from those where it first lived in. Natural selection in the stranded population leads to the thriving of individuals with features best suited to new conditions, and their features becoming most common. Even random genetic changes concentrated in a small group can change dominant characteristics. This is called "genetic drift." Eventually, a new species emerges.

480,000–350,000 YEARS AGO

Polar bears evolved from brown bears when ice spread through part of the area where the bears lived. Growing white fur to hide in the snow, as well as a thick layer of fat beneath the skin to keep them warm, enabled the bears to survive in colder conditions than their near relatives.

Neanderthals used tools and fire, made art, buried their dead, and possibly used language.

450–400,000 YEARS AGO

Neanderthals emerged as the humans living in Europe. They survived until around 40,000 years ago, after the arrival of *Homo sapiens*.

315,000 YEARS AGO

Homo sapiens evolved in Africa. Modern humans have changed little in their physical and mental abilities from their first *Homo sapiens* ancestors.

Homo sapiens became a top predator through the use of tools and cooperation with others.

About 300,000 years ago, much of Europe and North America was covered with forest. The temperature and sea level were about the same as they are today, and carbon dioxide levels were the same as they were before the rapid rise in fossil fuel use. Modern humans evolved to live in a climate and with landmasses similar to today's world.

300,000 YEARS AGO

Megaloceros was 3 m (10 ft) tall to the tip of the antlers and 3 m (10 ft) long.

400,000–95,000 YEARS AGO

Megaloceros was a **giant deer** with the largest antlers of any animal that has ever lived. These animals weren't all big, though. Some *Megaloceros* that lived on islands grew to less than 100 cm (39 in) tall. Animals that live on an island sometimes stay small. This prevents them from eating so much that they run out of food on the island and become extinct. It's called **"insular dwarfism."**

300,000 YEARS AGO

Neanderthals used **wooden spears**, long-distance weapons that meant they could hunt and kill larger prey than they could have tackled at short range. For example, it is difficult to approach a horse close enough to kill it with a handheld weapon, but they could kill a it from a distance with a spear. This gave them an advantage over other predators.

Wooden spear points were often hardened in a fire.

400,000 YEARS AGO

Early humans started using **fire** consistently. They could use it to defend themselves against predators, to harden weapons, and to cook food. Fire use increased rapidly around 300,000 years ago.

300,000—80,000 YEARS AGO

The world was warmer than now, and animals currently found near the equator lived farther north. Elephants lived in Germany, and hippos lounged in the River Thames in England. But the warmth didn't last. Ice has come and gone 25 times over the last 2.5 million years, with the most recent glacial period starting 126,000 years ago.

300,000 YEARS AGO

The Australian *Meiolania* was possibly the **largest land turtle** that ever lived. It couldn't draw its head into its shell to protect itself because of the spikes on its head—but the spikes protected *Meiolania* against the bite of predators.

Some *Meiolania* had a shell 2 m (7 ft) long, but on islands many reached only 70 cm (28 in).

126,000—12,000 YEARS AGO

Giant tapirs lived in China and Indonesia. Although a tapir's nose looks like a shortened elephant trunk, the tapir is more closely related to the horse and rhinoceros.

Giant tapir, 3.5 m (11.4 ft) long

300,000 YEARS AGO

250,000—24,000 YEARS AGO

Cave bears, despite their large size, ate mostly plant food, but possibly scavenged dead meat occasionally. Their need to hibernate held dangers: Some seem to have been killed while sleeping in their caves by cave lions.

Cave bear, 3 m (10 ft) long

125,000 YEARS AGO

Neanderthals used fire to clear forest in the region that is now Germany, showing that humans have a **significant impact on the environment**. No other organism has deliberately changed the environment on such a scale.

100,000—50,000 YEARS AGO

A **small species of human** called *Homo floresiensis* lived in Indonesia and grew to only 110 cm (43 in) tall.

110,000 YEARS AGO

The **Mammoth Steppe** developed, stretching from Spain to eastern Russia and into Alaska and Canada. At the time, it was Earth's largest biome (collection of living organisms in an environment). It lasted 100,000 years and was home to megafauna including Steppe bison, horses, and mammoth that fed on grass and low-growing shrubs. Although cold and dry, it was as rich in animal and plant life as an African savanna is today.

Steppe bison, 2 m (6.5 ft) long, evolved around 600,000 years ago, but came into their own on the Mammoth Steppe and survived until 5,000 years ago.

90,000 YEARS AGO

People in land that is now the Democratic Republic of Congo used **barbed points made of bone** to spear fish.

80,000 YEARS AGO

100,000 YEARS AGO

Homo sapiens left Africa to begin **spreading around the world**. They started to affect other living things in every environment they went into.

Modern humans evolved in Africa and spread from there around the world.

100,000 YEARS AGO

The human **body louse** first appeared—evidence that humans began to wear clothes. The lice live not directly on the body, but in clothing.

Body louse, 2.5–3.5 mm (0.1 in) long

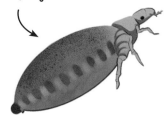

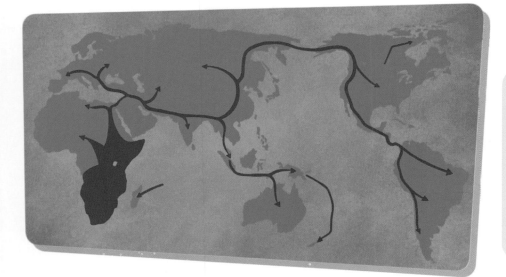

85,000 YEARS AGO

The first evidence of modern humans **using fire systematically to change the landscape** comes from Malawi in Africa. Here, people cleared forest by burning trees, apparently deliberately changing the types of plants and animals that lived in the area.

A WORLD SHAPED BY ICE

The climate changed around 126,000 years ago, starting a glacial period that would last more than 100,000 years. The cold was most intense about 20,000 years ago. At that time, the global temperature was around 6° C (11° F) lower than it is now, and rainfall was half of current levels. This period ended 11,700 years ago when Earth settled into its current climate.

FROZEN LANDS

Nearly a third of Earth's surface (30 per cent) was **covered with ice** all year round 18,000 years ago. Some of it was 3.2 km (2 miles) thick. In the south, ice sheets stretched from Antarctica into Argentina, and in the north they spread across North America, northern Europe— including all of the British Isles and down to the Alps—and in patches across Siberia in northern Russia. Glaciers covered the Andes in South America and appeared in New Zealand, Tasmania, and the mountains of east and central Africa. Where the land wasn't covered with ice, lakes formed in the summer from the meltwater running off glaciers.

MORE LIVING SPACE

During the coldest spells, sea levels fell to 120 m (400 ft) below current levels since so much water was locked up in ice. This level revealed land that was previously submerged, making **land bridges** that allowed animals and plants to spread between regions usually separated by sea. The English Channel (between England and France) was dry, and the sea between eastern Russia and Alaska disappeared, leaving a land bridge called Beringia.

With dry land between Britain and Continental Europe, animals including humans could walk freely between them.

Current land

Extra land exposed 20,000 years ago

The woolly rhino, *Coelodonta*, lived throughout Europe and Asia for 2.5 million years, until 14,000 years ago.

WILD AND WOOLLY

To cope with the cold, **many animals grew large**. There were already many megafauna—animals had been growing large for some time. But the megafauna of the ice lands were often even larger. A large body size helps an animal to keep warm. Animals like the woolly rhinoceros had a thick coat of fur and layers of fat as insulation to help them keep warm, too. Over 3 m (10 ft) long, the woolly rhino had a hump on its back where it stored fat, built up in spring and summer, which helped to see it through the winter when the plants it ate died back and were hard to find under the ice.

Woolly mammoths thrived in the cold of the Mammoth Steppe.

SPARSE GRASS

The icy land was not forested, but grew **moss, lichens, and a few low-growing plants**. A few centimeters down, much of the ground was permanently frozen (called "permafrost"), making it impossible for trees to grow deep roots. Animals such as mammoths, deer, and woolly rhinos had to survive on the grasses and scrub. These plants grew freely in summer, but were hard to find in winter.

WINTRY LIVES

While megafauna grew thick fur and fat, humans used the pelts of animals they had killed to make **clothes** and lit **fires** to keep warm. They made **shelters** from sticks, bones, and the hides of animals they ate. They were the first organism that could use tools and ingenuity to overcome the challenges of living in a hostile environment.

We know the animals these humans lived among and hunted, because they left **cave art** showing them in carefully observed detail.

Cave paintings of spotted horses seem to show the real pattern of horses living alongside the artists.

Remains of shelters made of mammoth bones and hide show us how early humans lived in the cold.

10,000 BCE—NOW

Many of the changes over the last 12,000 years have been caused by the impact of humans. We have changed landscapes by clearing land to farm and build cities. We have changed individual organisms and changed the balance of nature. Here, dates less than 10,000 years ago are given in the form BCE and CE. After 1 BCE, the current era (CE) starts.

12,000 YEARS AGO

Humans began **farming**, choosing what to grow and clearing trees using tools and fire. By selective breeding (choosing which animals or plants to breed from), they changed the characteristics of farmed plants and animals.

By saving seed from the plumpest grains of corn (maize) to plant the next year, early farmers gradually changed corn from its wild form (left) to its modern form (right).

3000 BCE

The oldest living single tree, a **bristlecone pine**, sprouted in California.

10,000 BCE

6000—4000 BCE

The coral present now in the **Great Barrier Reef** started to grow when sea levels reached current levels 6,000 years ago. The sea became progressively deeper, new coral building on top of the old and so staying within the reach of sunlight as the reef grew taller.

2500 BCE

The last few **mammoths died out**, stranded on Wrangel Island off the northeast coast of Russia.

11,700–11,000 YEARS AGO

The end of the icy period **killed off large animals** that couldn't adapt to the new climate. North America was home to most megafauna, including all animals that weighed over 1,000 kg (2,200 lb). Animals including the giant beaver *Castoroides*, 2 m (7 ft) long, camels, mammoths, and mastodons all disappeared.

The Great Barrier Reef, off the eastern coast of Australia, is one of the most diverse marine habitats in the world. The reef itself is Earth's largest living structure.

2000 BCE

The oldest surviving **termite colonies** started in Africa and Brazil. Termites are social insects that first evolved around 200 million years ago. The colony works together as a "superorganism," with many sterile individuals carrying out tasks such as building and defending the colony, and a few fertile individuals breeding. The largest colony in Brazil is the size of Britain, made of 200 million mounds.

1519

Modern horses were reintroduced to North America from Europe by Hernán Cortés, who brought 16 of them for transport when he invaded Mexico. They had become extinct in America where they first evolved 11,000 years ago—but not before they had crossed the Bering Straits to live in Asia.

The dodo grew to 1 m (3.3 ft) tall

1662

The **dodo**, a flightless bird that lived on the island of Mauritius, was **driven to extinction** by human hunters, habitat destruction, and being preyed on by rats carried on sailing ships. This was the first time that the impact of humans on the disappearance of a species was recognized.

1000–1200 CE

The giant, flightless **elephant bird** was **driven to extinction** in Madagascar, probably by human activity.

Standing 3 m (10 ft) tall, the elephant bird was the world's heaviest-ever bird.

NOW

1936

The **last thylacine**, or Tasmanian tiger, **died**. Its extinction was the result of competition with wild dogs introduced to Tasmania from Europe, disappearance of its prey, destruction of its habitat, and epidemic disease.

Tasmanian tiger, 100–130 cm (36–51 in)

When humans take an organism into a new environment, it often becomes an invasive species. This means that it competes successfully with the organisms already living there, often taking over the habitat and damaging the ecosystem. Invasive species can be introduced on purpose—to grow or breed for food, for example—or by accident as stowaways on ships (rats) or in food (crop pests).

2023

The conservation plan for the **kākāpō**, a large, flightless parrot from New Zealand, is **a success**. There are now over 250 birds, up from 51 in 1995. The islands they live on are kept predator-free.

ON THE BRINK

Humankind has influenced on life on Earth for thousands of years now, but the impact has increased hugely over the last few hundred years. Now, our use of fossil fuels is also changing the climate rapidly. This will challenge not only us, but all the organisms with which we share the planet.

MOVING AROUND

People move around the planet freely, sailing over oceans and crossing vast continents. They have often taken plants and animals with them, introducing them into new environments. In 1859, European settlers released 13 rabbits into Australia, so that they could hunt them for sport. Rabbits breed quickly, so they soon devastated native plants and outcompeted native animals. By the late 1940s, there were 600 million rabbits in Australia. It was the fastest-ever spread of an **introduced species**. Humans have introduced rats and crop pests accidentally to new areas, and birds, horses, camels, rabbits, and many plants deliberately.

Rabbits took a terrible toll on Australian ecosystems.

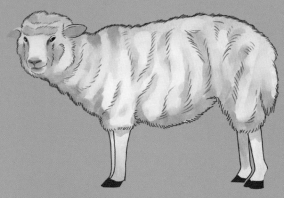

"Dolly" was the first mammal successfully cloned from a body cell of a single parent, in 1996.

CHANGING BODIES AND LIVES

As soon as people began farming, they changed the plants and animals they farmed. At first, they did this by choosing to breed from organisms with preferred features, but since the 1970s people have worked directly with the **genes** of plants and animals to tailor them to our tastes. Some of these changes are useful, such as adding extra vitamins to a crop. Others are whimsical, such as making day-glo pet fish. We can even make **clones**— exact copies—of an individual plant or animal.

The gray fritillary is harder to see than the original yellow flower. As gray flowers survive and reproduce, they become more common.

LIVING AROUND US

Some organisms have begun to **adapt to living around humans**. Some fish have started spawning at a smaller size, since large fish are caught by fishing fleets. Elephants have evolved smaller tusks, as large-tusked individuals have been targeted by poachers. Even plants have changed. The fritillary, a plant that grows on rocky slopes, is harvested as an ingredient in traditional medicine. Its flowers are changing from yellow to a hard-to-spot gray.

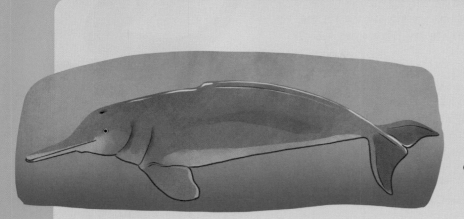

The last known river dolphin died in 2002.

PRESENT DANGER

Scientists believe that the next **mass extinction** has begun, caused by human activity. Already, 900 species have become extinct since 1500. Some animals have been driven to extinction by overhunting, by people destroying the places they live, or by introducing invasive species. In addition, we are causing severe **climate change**. Climate change has been a feature of all previous mass extinctions.

MAKING GOOD

It's not all bad news, though. In some areas, people are trying to **preserve and restore biodiversity**. They do this by protecting environments, preventing poaching, controlling pollution, and "rewilding" areas. Rewilding allows nature to take back the land. There is even a plan to restore part of the Mammoth Steppe—not with mammoths, but with the plants that once lived there, supporting modern herbivores and protecting the soil and atmosphere. Microbes and insects that have already evolved to eat plastic give hope that we might be able to remove the massive mountains of plastic that pollute land and sea.

Rewilding in the Carpathian mountains in Romania has seen wolves, bison, and eagles return.

ONLY EARTH?

So far, Earth is the only place we know in the universe that supports life. Astronomers seek signs of past or present **life elsewhere**, both in our own solar system and around distant stars. Perhaps the timeline of living things has played out many times in different times and places, and we might one day learn of very different forms of life.

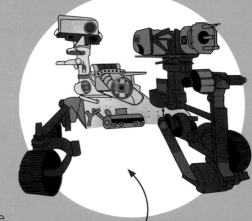

The NASA rover Perseverance is searching for evidence that microbes lived on Mars millions or billions of years ago.